# FACE

## TO

# FACE

**12** **Edgar Cayce Readings Interpreted for Today**

A.R.E.® PRESS • VIRGINIA BEACH • VIRGINIA

Reprinted from *Face to Face* (A.R.E. Press,
Virginia Beach, Va., 1982-1984)


Copyright © 1987
by the
Edgar Cayce Foundation.
All Rights Reserved.

ISBN 87604-200-0


Second Printing, February, 1988


Printed in the U.S.A.

# TABLE OF CONTENTS

# FOREWORD

The Edgar Cayce readings present an invitation and a promise—that each of us can come to know directly God within. This "face to face" encounter may be something we don't feel worthy of, and yet the opportunity is extended to each of us. One Cayce reading put it this way:

> **. . . the times and times and a half times shall pass, and _then_ shall man come to know that in the temple, in the tabernacle of his own temple will he meet his God face to face! 257-201**

There is a central idea in the physically derived information given by Cayce to individuals in his own times and now available to us all today. That universal idea is that we can each grow in spiritual maturity. Although we may start out our spiritual studies much like children starting out physical life, development is possible. And as we mature, old ways disappear and new understandings emerge. Isn't this just what the Apostle Paul meant when he wrote:

> "When I was a child, I spake as a child, I understood as a child, I thought as a child: but when I became a man, I put away childish things. For now we see through a glass, darkly; but then face to face . . ."
>
> I Corinthians 13:11-12

Cayce's life work was to help individual people move from seeing "through a glass, darkly" to seeing "face to face." Each reading was an invitation to see life in a new way and to apply in some practical fashion that maturing spiritual insight. Many people—those who received personal readings _and_ those who have learned from readings given for others—have been led to directly experience God "face to face."

In this book there is collected for you, the seeker, 12 of Cayce's best readings. They have been picked in such a way as to represent the broad scope of his material. They are readings which spoke profoundly to those who originally received them, but which also have applicability to us for today.

The source of the Cayce readings was special in many ways, but one particularly important quality was its capacity to present timeless wisdom. While addressing the immediate needs and questions of people in Cayce's own times, the readings also presented universal laws and principles which are just as true and useful in our own times.

Each of the 12 readings in this book comes with an interpretive commentary—an essay that offers insights about the meaning of that reading and how it is relevant to today's world with its own special set of challenges. The material in this book is a reprint collection of home-study materials published sequentially over a two-year period for members of the Association for Research and Enlightenment, Inc. So many people reported enthusiastically on how this material had helped them move closer to a "face to face" encounter with God that a republication seemed appropriate. Twelve of the original twenty-four topics are included here.

As you read and apply the ideas in this book, be sure to make use of both of its features: the interpretive commentaries *and* the full text of 12 Cayce readings. Don't miss studying the readings themselves. Most previous publications dealing with the Cayce material have included in their texts only brief excerpts from the readings. Many people who have "studied the Cayce readings" through books, articles and lectures have never encountered an *entire* reading. Whereas there may be considerable benefit from the wise selection of key excerpts, there is another kind of positive experience for the spiritual seeker who reads in its entirety a Cayce reading, just as it was given.

This book, which is the product of Edgar Cayce's own creativity and that of five contemporary students of his work, provides you with several kinds of "face to face" opportunity. First is the chance to encounter directly the Cayce readings just as they were given. Second, as you study these lessons in spiritual law and apply them, you will have a "face to face" encounter with yourself—perhaps in ways you never have before. And most important, by living the ideas found in this book you will take a step in spiritual maturity toward that time when you no longer "see through a glass, darkly" but instead meet your God "face to face."

Mark A. Thurston, Ph.D.
Editor

# FACE

## TO

# FACE

# THE WORK

## by Herbert Bruce Puryear, Ph.D.

In the beginning as children of God, we worked and played, loved, created and communicated face to face with the Father. However, as we are told in the Genesis account, we experienced ourselves driven out from the face of the Father.

Then, it was first Jacob who, after wrestling all night with an angel of the Lord, said of himself, "I have seen God face to face . . ." (Genesis 32:30) After that it was Moses of whom it is said, repeatedly, that he spoke with God face to face.

This great event is promised again in Ezekiel. The Lord instructs the prophet in a spirit almost of dismay with respect to His children, that He "will bring you into the wilderness of the people, and there will I plead with you face to face." (Ezekiel 20:35) It is as though the Father continues to seek out His children in a confrontation and awareness of Him that is characterized by this great expression and promise: face to face.

In the Corinthians chapter on love, the apostle Paul says, ". . . now we see through a glass darkly; but then face to face . . ." (I Corinthians 13:12) Much has been made of the first part of this statement, "through a glass darkly"; however, little encouragement has been advanced regarding the immediacy of the second part, the experience of "face to face." We think of this as something that may take place in some distant future. However, the Edgar Cayce readings assure us ". . . that His promises are sure, that there may come that life in a manifested form that would begin again those of face to face may they speak with the Father and with the Son." (254-68)

The time in which there may "begin again those of face to face" is at hand! We are in need of such a consciousness at many levels *now*. We need to come face to face with ourselves as spiritual beings and how we resist full awareness of the Godhead within. We need to come face to face with what is happening in the world and with the implications of these current events. We need to come face to face with the role that we may, indeed must, play in bringing light into a world in need. Thus we need to come face to face with our soul's purpose, that work for which we entered this very incarnation. Most of all, we need to commit ourselves, prepare ourselves to come face to face with God, our Father.

Those of us who are enthusiastic about the work and readings of Edgar Cayce as an aid and encouragement to these tasks need also to be willing to come face to face with this information which is purported to come from the Universal Source. Many of us have become convinced not only of the documentation and authenticity but also of the helpfulness of this information. And yet even *we* have not availed ourselves of the opportunity to experience these readings in the depth which they warrant: a face-to-face study of the Spirit which they reveal.

Some people claim they do not "understand" the readings. Others are bothered by the archaic language in them. Yet, by failing to come face to face with what this information says, we may be failing to avail ourselves of the opportunity to experience manifestations of the very Spirit of the living God.

Therefore, let us put aside any sense of inhibition or hindrance or reluctance and let us address these readings directly. It is hoped that these commentaries will enhance the study of them in such a way that you may not only better comprehend but also come to feel competent and movitated to continue studying the readings.

If we find it in ourselves to approach this task with a high spirit, we may find greater aid than anticipated in coming face to face with the true issues of life: our relationship to God, to our fellow human beings, and to our soul's purpose and life work in this incarnation.

## The Work

This work, what is it about? It may be that the greater the scope of the work, the more difficult it is for us to obtain or maintain a proper perspective on it. Also, it may be that the greater the work, the simpler its ideals and purposes might become. Nevertheless, the far-reaching implications may be so expansive as to seem beyond our day-to-day lives, especially regarding what seem to be overwhelming events on a worldwide scale.

What is the purpose of this work? There were literally hundreds of occasions on which questions were asked about the nature of the work and on which the source of these readings gave comments or discourses. A consistency of spirit and purpose can be traced throughout all of these responses. This purpose may be found embedded in any or all of them; however, it is expressed in many different wordings. The great statement of purpose of this work is the same as that expressed by the Master in His presentation of the ultimate agenda of all mankind: It is the great commandment, love of God and neighbor.

If this pattern—in the form of the great commandment—is kept in mind throughout our study of the readings, it will be found again and again. We continue to be called to a re-examination of the implications of this law. Thus, it is the clear motto, ideal and purpose of this work, ". . . to make manifest the love of God and man; man's relation to man; man's relation to God. In *this* there must come, as has ever been given, success in such terms as the service is meted; and there may be expected that wholehearted cooperation from the Divine, in the mental and the *purely material,* in the same relation as the *wholeheartedness* is to the oneness of purpose! A divided house *cannot* stand." (254-42)

Now, from these hundreds of statements on the nature and purpose of this work, let us study one entire discourse given on this subject. The occasion was a scheduled reading given to the members of the Association at the Fourth Annual Congress in Virginia Beach, Va., on June 30, 1935. The reading number is 254-87. (See reading following this commentary.)

When examining an Edgar Cayce reading, it is very important for you to study carefully the wording of the suggestion given by the conductor prior to the beginning of the discourse. On this occasion the members in attendance desired to bring spiritual enlightenment to others, and they asked for a discourse on "how we may best present these truths to others." This question is of the utmost importance

---

3

to all of us who have become interested in this information and want to apply it.

In what spirit and in what manner may we best share with others what we have gained from this remarkable source? In this reply through the channel of Edgar Cayce, we are told "this might be answered in the one sentence, 'As ye have received, so give.'" The work is very simple: If something has brought you to a closer understanding of the Divine within, then out of the abundance of that experience, give likewise to others who seek. This is an amazing and beautiful and simple statement of this great work.

We are then encouraged to work with one purpose, one aim, one desire, yet each in his own way and manner, and are warned "though someone may laugh or scoff at what ye say, *be* not dismayed; for so did they at thy Lord." Remember the statement of the Master in the beatitude, "Blessed are ye, when men shall revile you, and persecute you . . . for my sake." (Matthew 5:11) How rarely do we claim that blessing, or how often do we let it slip by when we are reviled and persecuted? Do we not for lack of the right spirit fail to receive the promised blessing? How often do we fail to share that which has been helpful to us which might, to our surprise, be beneficial to another, because we are fearful of being scorned, rejected, persecuted?

Then we are told, "What ye *find* to do, with willing hands, DO ye." Although this is familiar advice for us all, we may not have sensed the deeper lawfulness of our need, in our own proper place and with our own special abilities, to make an appropriate input into the circumstances of the moment in which we lawfully find ourselves. These opportunities, rather than being by chance, are specific occasions for each of us to bring the manifestation of the Spirit into the earth in that particular finite manner. Then we are warned, "*realizing* that each and every chain is only as strong as the weakest link. Thou art a portion. Hast thou fulfilled, *wilt* thou fulfill, that as is shown thee by thine own *experience* with same?"

The individual likened to a link in a chain is a very instructive analogy. However, it may also be misleading if we think that every link in the chain is identical. Each is unique and has a unique purpose, and when the greater work of all the parts is considered, much may be lost when *anyone* fails to fulfill his portion. As we come face to face with this challenge and its implications for ourselves, we see that in a very specific way and manner we have a work to do in the place, time, and circumstance in which we find ourselves.

How are we to know exactly of what our own individual work consists? "ACT! Act as thy conscience and thy heart dictate; as thou hast received, so give." And we are invited to remember, "man may make *all* efforts, all activity, but only the Spirit of Truth, only God may give the increase . . ." As each of us then does what is at hand, a little leaven leavens the whole lot and the great work in the world is accomplished.

In many readings, after an introductory discourse, the source paused and said, "Ready for questions." Just as the wording of the suggestion given by the conductor was of great importance in what was subsequently given, so the wording of the questions presented to the source was all-important to what followed. In this case the questions were so carefully worded and so consistent in theme that it is worth examining them as a group to prepare ourselves to recognize the underlying principles that may be revealed in the responses. We want both to identify major themes and principles and also to look for special statements that constitute nuggets or, as we sometimes say, "goodies," imbedded in the readings.

The five questions asked are consistent in spirit with the initial suggestion regarding how to present the truths in the readings to others. First:

## 1. *What should be the central purpose, the central ideal in presenting the work?*

The answer to this first question is lengthy; it begins, "The Truth that shall make you free in body, in mind, and one *with* the living force that may express itself in *individual* lives." This statement of purpose is reminiscent of one of the well-known teachings of Jesus who said, "If ye continue in my word, then are ye my disciples indeed; And ye shall know the truth, and the truth shall make you free." (John 8:31-32)

This allusion to the Scripture and the teaching of the Master about Truth is a type of statement that frequently appears in the readings. If we respond appropriately, we have the opportunity for such a statement to be enriched by all that we know about the Bible and the mission of Jesus. Such a statement in the readings identifies the purpose and ideal of the work with that of the Master. This becomes especially clear in the closing paragraph of this answer.

> **You who feel that you are of little help here or there, or in manner of giving expression in thy words of mouth, then so live that ye have received that Spirit of Truth—*not* of any body but of Truth, or Christ—may be manifested. And those seeing—though ye struggle with the cares of earth, the cares of life—will, too, take hope and find in thine effort, in thine endeavor—though stumbling it may be—HOPE, and find the face of Him who has set a way for all who will enter in, who will sit at last upon that judgment within thine self. For, "As ye have done it unto the least of these, ye have done it unto me."**

Notice the way in which this response picks up on the earlier emphasis upon each individual fulfilling his or her portion. Each of us—even though we may feel that we are of little help here or there—may, as we live what we have received, bring hope to others, stumbling though our efforts may be. In closing we are challenged again with the words of the Master in the Olivet discourse, Matthew 24 and 25, in the great imagery of the separation of the sheep from the goats. The reading suggests that it is not God who judges us. We judge ourselves as we stand by that criterion of judgment set in the pattern of the Christ. "As ye have done it unto the least of these, ye have done it unto me."

Each of us has an important job to do in living the Spirit of Truth. Even if we stumble, we may in our efforts bring *hope* to others; and as we do unto those who are the *least* in our own estimation, we do unto the Christ.

This principle that His way, the Truth, will make us free is no doubt *the most difficult* lesson that we rebellious souls have to learn. We think *our* way will make us freer than the Truth. Only in pain and suffering may some of us learn that His way truly is our own proper way even to freedom and out of the bondage of our own making.

## 2. Should we try to inform or teach children about spiritual enlightenment, or merely show the way by example?

Now as to the manner in which we may work with our

children, the answer comes as no surprise: "By precept *and* example." And he adds that principle which should be so self-evident to us and yet which may be so problematic for all of us in our work with our children: ". . . do not say one thing and live another!" In another context these readings indicate that nothing hinders more than speaking in one manner and living in another. This is an example of a kind of universal truth often found in the readings which we may slide over because it sounds so familiar. We may fail to recognize it as a spiritual law. Could it be that a major problem at the national as well as the personal level in teaching our children is saying one thing and living another? And could it be, if it matters to us, that we could make a significant contribution to the national problem by beginning to live in the manner in which we are trying to teach our children?

### 3. *How should we present the work to one in orthodox faith?*

The last three questions deal with the presentation of the work to people of different persuasions. The answer points to the spirit in which we approach and share with another. "*Come* and *see!* In *that* manner." Too often we are anxious or defensive about what we have to share, and in our anxiety we come off as being overly enthusiastic; the potential recipient feels imposed upon. We are invited to remember that only those who are in need will heed.

A very serious indictment is levied against those who are satisfied in their present limited understanding. "If they are satisfied in their own mire, or their own vomit, then do not disturb. For only the *Father* may quicken." This strong language alludes to several Biblical passages which may be illustrated in this: "But it is happened unto them according to the true proverb, The dog is turned to his own vomit again; and the sow that was washed to her wallowing in the mire." (II Peter 2:22)

Such allusions to the Scriptures should invite the serious student to turn to a Bible concordance, locate and study carefully the context from which the quotation is taken. For example, in this case the whole of II Peter 2 might be studied as background for a better appreciation of the enriched context of this expression.

Nevertheless, in spite of the strong language, an attitude which we should hold toward those who have ideas different from our own prevails: "If ye would find and know mercy before Him, be merciful and kind to those in whatever faith or whatever group ye may find them."

## 4. What should be the approach to one who has become interested in cults, isms, etc.?

The principle of "Come and see" is picked up again and amplified in this response: "In that same manner; for what is the difference?" This "what is the difference?" is a startling answer for those of us who think of our own orientation as "orthodox" in contrast to those whom we may accuse of being in cults or "isms." The source of the readings does not differentiate between them. This may be worth serious reflection, especially if we identify positively with one expression of the work and find ourselves critical of another expression. Then is given a beautiful illustration and analogy to clarify this principle:

> **Are there not trees of oak, of ash, of pine? There are the needs of these for meeting this or that experience. Hast thou chosen any one of these to be the *all* in thine usages in thine own life?**
> **Then, all will fill their place. Find not fault with *any*, but rather show forth as to just how good a pine, or ash, or oak, or *vine*, thou art!**

This response makes it very clear that God has a place for different manifestations and structures in the order of humanity, and it also suggests that no one of these should be considered as able to fulfill all the needs of any individual. It also makes clear that the question is not whether others should be in the form or work or church which *we* prefer, but rather the question is, How good are we in that form that we have chosen?

Let us examine this a step further. A portion of this answer is ". . . it will ever be found that Truth—whether in this or that schism or ism or cult—is of the One source." This statement is very similar to one of the statements of the purpose of Atlantic University, chartered as a portion of this work in 1931. One of these readings indicates that a purpose of the University is to take that which *is truth* from every ism, schism, and clime and adapt it so that it may aid those who would be of service to others. Applicable truths can be found in many schisms and isms, illustrating the universality of the readings' view that all of us are children of God and that God is in a measure working with and through everyone in every land, in every time. Further, it is suggested that we may extract insights from these other forms which can aid us in the ideal of service to others.

A personal attitude that may be derived from this more universal approach is that, if we as seekers are willing to listen, we may learn from others, whatever their orientation or persuasion. Perhaps those of whom we think the least might have something which, were we willing to listen, would help us to help others.

## 5. How should we present it to one who has lost faith in Creative Force?

The answer, "Live it!" As we live it, we enable that one through a material expression to take cognizance of the truth that is going on about him. We are told that in so doing we may "heap upon the head of him who has denied faith, who has denied the Lord, that which will make a call or desire for a change . . ."

This gem gives us a key to interpreting a rather enigmatic principle given both in Proverbs 25:21-22 and Romans 12:20. For example, in Romans we are told, "Therefore if thine enemy hunger, feed him; if he thirsts, give him drink: for in so doing thou shalt heap coals of fire on his head." The Biblical imagery of heaping coals of fire on the head may not sound like a loving thing to do; however the readings' interpretation of this indicates that it may have the effect of creating a desire for a change. In other words, when we live the truth and demonstrate it before those who have lost faith, they take cognizance of the truth being enacted before them, for a desire for change has been created in them, and "*then* ye may point the way that has been helpful, hopeful to thee."

And last, a final benediction:

**Be not overcome with those things that make for discouragements, for *He* will supply the strength. Lean upon the arm of the Divine within thee, giving not place to thoughts of vengeance or discourage- ments. Give not vent to those things that create prejudice. And, most of all, be UNSELFISH! For selfishness is sin, before first thine self, then thine neighbor and thy God.**

**Love ye one another. Give as ye have received.**

This is the kind of passage that is worth reading and rereading, reflecting upon to write, as it were, these truths in permanent form upon our own hearts and consciences. As we address this as a work of the great commandment to love God and our neighbor, we find in this reading some extraordinary advice and insights regarding how to go about sharing with others that which we have received ourselves. If we will study these words more carefully and let the Truth quicken our hearts, we may find a new sense of helpfulness and purpose in our relationships with all with whom we come in contact. And we may find ourselves meeting *Him*, face to face.

# Reading Number 254-87 ____

*This psychic reading given by Edgar Cayce at his home on Arctic Crescent, Virginia Beach, Va., June 30, 1935, in accordance with request made by those present at the final meeting of the Fourth Annual Congress of the Association for Research and Enlightenment, Inc. . . .*

Mrs. Cayce: *You will have before you the interest of this group, present in this room, in aiding in bringing spiritual enlightenment to others, and the way opened through presenting the psychic work of Edgar Cayce through the Association for Research and Enlightenment, Inc. You will give a discourse on how we may best present these truths to others, and will answer the questions that may be asked.*

Mr. Cayce: Yes, we have the group as gathered here, as a group, as individuals; and their interest in how they may be of aid or help to their fellow man.

In giving that as might be helpful to each, in presenting the truths of a spiritual nature as come through the channel here of Edgar Cayce, this might be answered in the one sentence, "As ye have received, so give." If that which has been thine experience has brought thee to a closer understanding of the Divine within, whether from the physical, the mental or the spiritual approach to this work, then of the abundance of thine own experience give out to those that seek; that they, too, may be filled in their own way and manner.

For He has promised, and His promises are sure, "What ye ask in my name, *believing,* ye shall receive."

Many are the channels, as are the minds, of those gathered here. Many make their approach in the manner in which they as individuals have heard, have experienced, have received.

Then all with one purpose, one aim, one desire, yet in their own *way* and manner, should present that they have received. And though someone may laugh or scoff at what ye say, *be* not dismayed; for so did they at thy Lord.

As to manners or ways as a collective group: What ye *find* to do, with willing hands DO ye. This may to thine own mind, then, appear to be very indefinite, intangible. Yet is there not set in the experience of each that through some specific office, through some specific group as a part of a working unit, there is specific work set for that unit?

As an individual, then, do thy part; *realizing* that each and every chain is only as strong as the weakest link. Thou art a portion. Hast thou fulfilled, *wilt* thou fulfill, that as is shown thee by thine own *experience* with same?

What *is* the manner, the way that thou shouldst choose? As He has given, and as ye would ever hear and know, if and when ye love one another even as He hath loved you, then thou wilt be, thou hast been, thou art shown the way. Not that any dictum is set! For He hath made thee to choose; and has said, "When ye call, I will hear—when ye are my children, *I* will be thy God."

So, as the work goes about in its various phases and channels to give help, aid, to this or that phase of its activities, and thou as an individual art called, or thou as an individual art impressed or feel that thou art called, then ACT! Act as thy conscience and thy heart dictate; as thou has received, so give.

Thus may ye accomplish that which is set before you as a group, as an organization, as an individual.

For unless thy heart, thine mind, is in that ye would do, naught can come to thine efforts. For *this* is the law; as ye sow, so shall ye reap. For man may make *all* efforts, all activity, but only the Spirit of Truth, only God may give the increase, the result. For He *is* the life, He *is* Truth. As ye give expression of same in thine experiences, in those channels, in those promises, in those places of thine *daily* activity, the results only then can and will and do become manifested in the lives and experiences and expressions of those ye contact, as an activative and motivative influence.

For remember ever, the little leavening that ye do day by day leavens the whole lot.

So, let thine mind, thine heart, thine body, be given in *that* manner in which ye have received; so give ye to thy fellow man.

Ready for questions.

**Q-1.** *What should be the central purpose, the central ideal in presenting the work?*

**A-1.** The Truth that shall make you free in body, in mind, and one *with* the living force that may express itself in *individual* lives.

Where there is illness of body, then give that which may make it free from those adaptings of itself *to* that which has bound it in this material expression.

Where there are those troubled in mind, with many cares, if they are seeking for the *spiritual* way, they, too, may find *how* in their *own* experience they may give the greater expression *their* application of that they have in hand.

Where there are those who seek for the channel in which they may be the greater expression in this material plane in the present experience, they, too, may find their own selves and *their* relationships to the holy within.

*These* should be the central themes. As to the choice of this or that manner to be used, follow the manners which have been set through which individual groups here and there may receive enlightenment or aid in a better understanding or concept of what such information is that may be supplied through such a channel, and how it is of help. These are being opened.

Those that are seeking for channels to aid those who in body have become under the bond of this or that affliction, this or that ill or ailment, may stress this particular line of endeavor in their activity. And some who are already aiding in such directions will soon seek the concept of some that are here. Give expression in mind. As ye have received, give out.

You who feel that you are of little help here or there, or in manner of giving expression in thy words of mouth, then so live that ye have received that Spirit of Truth—*not* of any body but of Truth, or Christ—may be manifested. And those seeing—though ye struggle with the cares of earth, the cares of life—will, too, take hope and find in thine effort, in thine endeavor—though stumbling it may be—HOPE, and find the face of Him who has set a way for all who will enter in, who will sit at last upon that judgment within thine self. For, "As ye have done it unto the least of these, ye have done it unto me."

**Q-2.** *Should we try to inform or teach children about spiritual enlightenment, or merely show the way by example?*

**A-2.** By precept *and* example. More and more will there be that preparation. For in the present, as we have given, the more oft is the mind of the young trained to the material rather than to the spiritual! But in thine training do not say one thing and live another!

**Q-3.** *How should we present the work to one in orthodox faith?*

**A-3.** *Come* and *see!* In *that* manner. Not as imposing, not as impelling, but to all, "Come and see." For only those that are in need of the answering of something within will heed. If they are satisfied in their own mire, or their own vomit, then do not disturb. For only the *Father* may quicken. But so live in thine *own* life, in thine own associations; not finding fault. For if thy Father, God, had found fault with every idle word or every unkind act in thine experiences, what opportunity would *ye* have had in this experience?

If ye would find and know mercy before Him, be merciful and kind to those in whatever faith or whatever group ye may find them.

Oft ye will find, if ye so live, that others may say, "What has caused you to do this or that?" Not as a crank, not as one bereft of this or that. Live even as He, in thine social life, in thine home life, in thine business life, in thine own expessions everywhere, in such a way and manner as to bespeak that which thou would have thy God, thy Christ, to do or to be to thee.

**Q-4.** *What should be the approach to one who has*

*become interested in cults, isms, etc.?*

**A-4.** In that same manner; for what is the difference? As He has given, it will ever be found that Truth—whether in this or that schism or ism or cult—is of the One source. Are there not trees of oak, of ash, of pine? There are the needs of these for meeting this or that experience. Hast thou chosen any one of these to be the *all* in thine usages in thine own life?

Then, all will fill their place. Find not fault with *any*, but rather show forth as to just how good a pine, or ash, or oak, or *vine*, thou art!

**Q-5.** *How should we present it to one who has lost faith in Creative Force?*

**A-5.** Live it! For that in the material world is the manner in which each soul, whether in this or that thought, takes cognizance of that about it. In so doing, as He has said, ye heap upon the head of him who has denied faith, who has denied the Lord, that which will make a call or desire for a change; and *then* ye may point the way that has been helpful, hopeful to thee.

Be not overcome with those things that make for discouragements, for *He* will supply the strength. Lean upon the arm of the Divine within thee, giving not place to thoughts of vengeance or discouragements. Give not vent to those things that create prejudice. And, most of all, be UNSELFISH! For selfishness is sin, before first thine self, then thine neighbor and thy God.

Love ye one another. Give as ye have received.

We are through for the present.

COME, my children! Bow thine heads! For I would BLESS thee in thine choice!

254-87

# THE MISSION OF THE SOUL

## by Herbert Bruce Puryear, Ph.D.

The Edgar Cayce readings view a person as a physical, mental and spiritual being. As an individual entity, each of us has a physical body, a mental body and a spiritual body, which is the soul. It is well known that of the more than 14,000 psychic discourses given by Edgar Cayce some 8,000 deal with the physical body. It is not as well known that there were also several hundred readings which are called mental-spiritual readings. These deal with considerations of the mental body and the soul body of the recipient of the reading. Some of the finest and most helpful instructions for understanding ourselves mentally and spiritually may be found in these extraordinary discourses. In some respects these readings, in dealing with mental and spiritual laws, may have a wider general applicability for every reader than do most of the physical readings, which deal with very specific disorders.

The reading for our present consideration, 442-3, given for a 57-year-old-man, is an excellent example of this kind of information. These mental-spiritual readings designate us as souls, children of God, with a mission to be accomplished in the present incarnation. This mission is based upon previous sojourns of the soul in this and other planes of consciousness, especially with respect to the ideals and purposes held by the entity and the application made in those previous experiences with respect to the ideals or criteria being held by the individual.

Frequently in such readings the expression is given that "the entity gained, the entity lost." Although this wording is not used in 442-3, it is indicated that there were retarding influences due to indecisions and engaging in particular activities. However, because application was made with respect to an ideal, the entity gained overall. That gain is specifically indicated as a growth "in patience." The information reminds us that it was:

> . . . by Him who is the Giver of life as being the qualification in every entity's experience through the application (of patience) every entity becomes aware of possessing a soul, that birthright which is the gift of the Father to each and every entity that may be presented before the Throne of thrones, before the Holy of holies . . .

The words, "In your patience possess ye your souls," are attributed to the Master in reference to what we might expect in the latter days. The readings' interpretation of this well-known expression indicates that possessing the soul involves becoming *aware* of possessing a soul. (Luke 21:19) And we are promised that this soul is to be presented before the Throne of thrones, before the Holy of holies, in a holy, acceptable way and manner.

> . . . the soul is that which is individual of each and every body as it finds expression in the material world, which lives on and on in those environs that have been created by what that soul has seen and comprehended in its experience as being according to those directions as He, the Father, the Lord of all, would have each and every soul be.

Here we are reminded of a principle, somewhat different from the teachings of many, that each and every *body* that finds expression in the material world has and is a *soul*. It is not that something additional is required by way of a certain kind of religious awakening or experience for the soul to be implanted in that body—one soul for every body and that soul lives on and on. In what kind of experience? We are told that the experiences are in "those environs that have been created by what that soul has seen and comprehended . . ."

We have talked much about heaven and hell but very little about the specific way we, as co-creators with God, are building by our thoughts, choices, activities, and ideals those kinds of experiences in consciousness into which we will move when we put aside the physical body. (442) is given encouragement that much that he has done is well pleasing in the eyes of God. We must understand and interpret this seriously to mean that God the Father does indeed have an awareness and concern about each and every one of His children.

There is another fascinating phrase that gives a quickening interpretation to an expression in the Bible. We have heard that he who endures unto the end shall wear the crown of life. Here the crown of life is interpreted as "being aware of those abilities within self to know that the self, the ego, the I, is in accord with, is aware of, the divine protection . . ." The crown of life then is an awareness. Here also the words, "self," "ego," and "I" are used synonymously. We must understand that words such as these do not have a fixed meaning and may be given alternate meanings by different sources in certain contexts. Sometimes the word *self* and the word *ego* are used to refer to the lower self. Here they seem to refer more to the individuality or higher self of the entity. (Failure to learn and keep in mind the specialized connotations given to words by differing sources may lead to confusion.)

Now let us consider this crown of life which comes with the awareness that the *I* "is in accord with, is aware of, the divine protection that has and does come to each and every soul that fulfills its mission in any experience." First, let us anticipate personally claiming this protection that is assured by resolving and seeking to be sure that we do fulfill our mission in this experience.

"What, then, ye ask, has been the mission of this entity, this soul, in this experience?" This soul's mission may be appropriate for and applicable in some considerable measure to each of us:

> **That, with that which has gone before, there may be given the opportunity as to what the soul would do about that it knows is in accordance with, in keeping with, what His injunctions have ever been to His fellow man . . .**

The mission of the soul then is the opportunity to do *what the soul knows to do* toward the fellow human being which is in accordance with the injunctions of the Lord.

What are these injunctions? Let us list them for clarity of understanding:

1. *That ye may make thy path straight.*
2. *That ye do unto others as ye would have others do unto you.*

17

3. *Love the Lord thy God.*
4. *Eschew evil.*
5. *Keep the heart joyous in the service and in the tasks that are set before thee day by day.*
6. *Do with a might in the Lord that thy hands find to do.*

Through living and keeping with these injunctions, we may grow in grace and in the knowledge and understanding of the Lord and His ways.

Now we may add a seventh: "Not that ye rest idly by when there is work to do, but just being kind, just being patient, just being long-suffering with those who would err according to thine own conscience . . ." Here we are invited to show forth the love and patience that the Lord "hast shown with the sons of men since He has called into being *bodies*—physically . . ."

We are told that the Lord has shown to each of us a very special and personal patience since He has created bodies for us. What is to be the purpose of these bodies? That they "may furnish a channel through which those things that are known and accepted as being the qualifications of a spiritual life may *find* manifestations, and thus bring forth their fruits, their meats, ready for repentance."

The Lord called physical bodies into being so that we might have a channel to give expression to the fruits of the spirit. In this assignment of manifesting the fruits of the spirit, we are invited to a joy and gladness for the opportunity to turn within in meditation and to claim the promise that in the silence we may be quickened by the Spirit and enabled to manifest those fruits of the spirit.

So often in these readings these fruits are described as "just being kind." Toward whom? Those "that have become and do become thy lot to be measured with. For, there are no such things as perchance . . ." Our families, our friends, our associates are not in relationships with us by chance, but rather that we are being *measured with* them in our experiences in the earth.

But how are we to measure others? The ultimate measurement of others to which we are so frequently enjoined is as given, "Inasmuch as ye have done it unto the least of these, my little ones, ye have done it unto me." We must then, as we measure others, see the Christ within them.

Now here is an interesting expression—"be acquainted with the Lord. Seek, in thy secret places, that He knoweth thee aright." This invites a familiarity with the Lord, an attitude of our approach to Him. Remember, when Jesus taught us to pray He used the word, *Abba*, which is frequently translated "Father," but more appropriately in the term of affection some express with the word, "Daddy." Unless we seek Him in secret places and practice the silence in meditation, the Lord may not know us aright! But as we are invited to seek His face, we are assured of His response and gifts of justice, mercy, peace, and harmony. His wish for each of us is *joy*. Then, there is reiterated again, that He would give us these four special fruits: mercy, peace, justice, and harmony.

As we set about doing what we find before us, we are assured that the Lord will call us by name. And when He names us there is nothing to fear save self.

The children of God may expect a personal response when we approach Him as Father. Only our own waywardness, indecision, and unkindness may keep us from this oneness. No power in heaven or earth, no principalities or other powers can separate the soul from the love of the Father except what we inflict upon ouselves.

Now (442) asks a question that is appropriate for all of us seekers on the spiritual path: "Is this entity one who may properly now pursue the higher and inner development of its soul and psychic forces?" The answer is one of encouragement. The instructions of this process involve some specific steps of preparation for the experience of meditation. And so the seeker is told to enter into the Holy of holies, first preparing by cleansing the mind and the body of whatever to the individual might be experienced as being unclean.

These instructions are given repeatedly in other readings as the first steps in meditation; and yet there is little clarity regarding them in the minds of many individuals who would meditate. Many are not clear about just what in their own conscience constitutes the kind of preparation that the readings express as being *clean* and ready for the approach to the Lord.

Many who came seeking a better understanding of which

forces might most properly guide them were told, as was this seeker, to be satisfied with nothing less than the Son or "those that He may guide." In these days with increasingly rapid psychic opening, we need to be carefully discerning of the spirits. There *are* tests which we may make. It may not suffice simply to ask, "Do you come in the name of the Christ?" and to receive a "Yes." The test should be more specific. The guides should be asked to articulate in their own words that, "Jesus Christ is my Lord and Master." Why turn to any other when He is so nigh? He has promised to answer. If He sends a messenger, that is fine, but the messenger must be evaluated. If the guide can say, "Jesus Christ is my Lord and Master," and if its work bears the fruit of the Spirit, then there is no problem.

The seeker is then given a beautiful prayer and affirmation: *Thy will, O God, be done in me as Thou seest I have need of, that I may be one with Thee—even as that I possessed with Thee before the world was.*

Why is the reference made to the former state instead of the future? Many, in seeking an approach to the Divine, have come in the spirit of desiring at some later date to be assured of entering heaven. This prayer reminds us of the parable of the prodigal son who *was with* the Father in the beginning, went astray of his own choice, came to himself and, "I will arise" to return. This important step of *remembering* from where we came is as important as knowing where we are going.

One of the purposes of the Edgar Cayce readings, as a book of remembrance, is to *remind* us. The expression, "as has been given," is not just to inform us that the source has already given us that information, but it is rather to call us to remember. Thus, the frequently reiterated expression, "as has been given," is also saying, "Remember, remember." We need to remember that we were with God in the beginning and that we went astray only because of our own choices. As this becomes clear, then we are enabled to come to ourselves and say, "I will arise." As we commit ourselves to returning, we are assured that He, our Father, will rush out, eagerly receive us, and restore to us our full inheritance.

Now the seeker in reading 442-3 is concerned that there may be influences in the physical and mental that would retard the soul in its development. He is assured that the attitude of God toward all His children is that if we will approach Him and place ourselves before the throne of grace and mercy, seeking Him in the silence within, then we will be guided as to what steps are needed to rid ourselves of anything that would deter us in the flesh.

As we are invited to approach the throne of grace, to turn to the Holy of holies within and to prepare ourselves, there may be warrings within the flesh. We are instructed to meet these conflicts in a step-by-step process. *Everything* that is given us may be put to use; and, as we use the opportunities presented to us, we grow in spirit and progress in our mission. As we put these gifts to use, they become bulwarks that prevent the carnal forces or other evil influences from intervening. *He* is all-powerful; and all other forces are helpless in His sight, for He is Lord of all. All power has been given Him in heaven and earth. This is our assurance of protection and in this we may be confident in being able to put aside those warring influences to approach Him within the temple of our own bodies.

The seeker is still in doubt and asks a couple of questions about karmic debt. He is assured, as the Cayce readings assure us all, that the Lord has prepared a way in which karmic influences may be met and that *way* is in the Christ taking these "debts" upon Himself. If karma is met in Him who is the Maker, the Creator, of all that exists, then day by day there is growth that is not deterred by *any* previous life influences.

**No karmic debts from other sojourns or experiences enter in the present that may not be taken away in that, "Lord, have Thy ways with me. Use me as Thou seest fit that I may be one with Thee."**

It is very important for us to learn about the law of karma. We must learn that we give account for every idle word. We need to understand the law in order to have a proper appreciation of the circumstances and conditions in which we find ourselves. We need to learn universal laws in order to understand how a loving God may permit His children to make choices and meet their consequences, even when they involve pain and suffering. However, one of the most important things that we may ever learn is that God does not record our karmic debts and hold against us something that must be repaid. It is rather that "like begets like" and "what we sow, we reap." However, as we meet ourselves in His spirit, the consequences are so tranformed that the outcome is entirely different. "Karmic debts" may be experienced as stepping-stones instead of stumbling blocks, and on occasion, indeed, blotted out. (See Acts 3:19, Isaiah 1:18.)

In a unique and specific question the seeker tries to understand the relationship of his previous life experiences in economic fields and yet his urge toward expression through art. The reading, in a delightful way, indicates that art and economics are related insofar as in art the soul seeks to give expression to the influences of nature itself which are indeed the closest manifestations of the love of a merciful father to a wayward son, and that in the study of this we also have an understanding of economics.

As the individual seeks a further understanding of previous life experiences, we are given a fascinating lesson on the relationship of experiences in the earth to experiences in other planes or spheres. It appears from this reading that experiences in other spheres, such as Mars, Mercury or Venus, feature "one particular activity." However, "in the earth we find *all* rolled into one, with a body and a body-mind for self-expression." Apparently, we meet the wholeness of ourselves more in the earth plane and we meet "specific activities" of ourselves in some of the other dimensions or planetary sojourns.

We may notice also a note of sober instruction that in Saturn we find the opportunity for "that cleansing that must come to all that have departed from the earth and have not kept the ways clean." Saturn is that planet or dimension into which all insufficient matter is cast for a remolding. (900-25) When we release the *flesh* body, there remains a "physical" body that may be in need of cleansing and the soul may choose to experience that cleansing in the purifying crucible of the Saturnian experience.

Earlier, (442) is given an extraordinary promise of specific kinds of ability related to art. Apparently, there is still hanging on a wall somewhere in a cave an artistic expression of the entity that is a "combination of all the periods into one." Artistic ability is further delineated in the contrast between the planetary experiences and the earth experiences in which "we find *all* rolled into one" and there seems to be an artistic talent of the soul that may enable him to do the visualization to give "expression in *all* of those things that may be found throughout the spheres."

And here is another of those unusual Biblical interpretations. When the Master said, "Other sheep I have that are not of this fold," the reading suggests that one interpretation may be that the other "folds" are those souls that sojourn in other spheres, or in the planetary sojourns between incarnations on the earth. They, too, may seek to hear His voice, to know His ways. What are these ways? Again, the fruits of the spirit, just being kind, just being patient, just loving one another, seeking to know and doing the will of the Father.

In this we are encouraged in the knowledge that we may walk and talk with God face to face and serve Him in our relationships with our fellow man. We may always be assured that He will be our guide, as we call upon Him throughout our mission in the earth.

What shall we then say to these things? If God be for us, who can be against us?

He that spared not his own Son, but delivered him up for us all, how shall he not with him also freely give us all things?

Who shall lay any thing to the charge of God's elect? It is God that justifieth.

Who is he that condemneth? It is Christ that died, yea rather, that is risen again, who is even at the right hand of God, who also maketh intercession for us.

Who shall separate us from the love of Christ? shall tribulation, or distress, or persecution, or famine, or nakedness, or peril, or sword?

As it is written, For thy sake we are killed all the day long; we are accounted as sheep for the slaughter.

Nay, in all these things we are more than conquerers through him that loved us.

For I am persuaded, that neither death, nor life, nor angels, nor principalities, nor powers, nor things present, nor things to come,

Nor height, nor depth, nor any other creature, shall be able to separate us from the love of God, which is in Christ Jesus our Lord.                    Rom. 8:31-39

# Reading Number 442-3 _____

*This psychic reading given by Edgar Cayce at the home of Mr. and Mrs. T. M. H. . . . Avenue, New York City, this 26th day of January, 1934, in accordance with request made by self—Mr. (442), Associate Member of the Association for Research and Enlightenment, Inc.*

*Suggestion: You will give a mental and spiritual reading for him, giving the reason for entrance into this cycle of experience and detailed guidance for the development and expression of his inner soul faculties in this present life. Questions:*

Mr. Cayce: Yes, we have the entity here, (442).

In considering the activities of the mental and soul body of an entity, in relations to its activities or its purposes in any given experience, something of that which has been builded in the soul development is necessary to be referred to as comparison, that there may be presented in a comprehensible way and manner that for mental and soul expansion in any given activity.

In this entity, (442), we find in the varied experiences or appearances through its activity in the environs, more of the developments than of retardments. While in varied experiences there are seen periods when indecisions and the particular activity made for rather the retarding, in the whole we have found that with the application of that which has become apparent in the present experience—as to what has been set as the ideals and principles by which the application of life in a given appearance or experience may be in a direction or in accordance with the entity's own judgments—the development has been in accord with an ideal. Making for, then, in self, patience—which has been pointed by Him who is the Giver of life as being the qualification in every entity's experience through the application of which every entity becomes aware of possessing a soul, that birthright which is the gift of the Father to each and every entity that may be presented before the Throne of thrones, before the Holy of holies, in a holy and acceptable way and manner.

In righteousness, then—as is found in patience, that has become the worthy attribute of the soul of this entity, in tolerance and in patience, has come the awareness of the continuity of life—and that the soul is that which is individual of each and every body as it finds expression in the material world, which lives on and on in those environs that have been created by what that soul has seen and comprehended in its experience as being according to those directions as He, the Father, the Lord of all, would have each and every soul be.

Then, as we find in the experiences of this entity, these have become worthy attributes, as these are well pleasing in His eyes; so that there may only be given that injunction, "Be not weary in well-doing, for he that endureth unto the end shall wear the crown of life." The crown of life here means being aware of those abilities within self to know that the self, the ego, the I, is in accord with, is aware of, the divine protection that has and does come to each and every soul that fulfills its mission in any experience.

What, then, ye ask, has been the mission of this entity, this soul, in this experience? That, with that which has gone before, there may be given the opportunity as to what the soul would do about that it knows is in accordance with, in keeping with, what His injunctions have ever been to His fellow man; that ye make thy paths straight, that ye do unto thy fellow man as ye would have your fellow man do unto you; love the Lord thy God, eschewing evil, keeping the heart joyous in the service and in the tasks that are set before thee day by day, doing with a might in the Lord that thy hands find to do. For, His ways have ever been that ye grow in the grace and in the knowledge and in the understanding of the Lord and His ways. Not that ye rest idly by when there is work to do, but just being kind, just being patient, just being long-suffering with those who would err according to thine own conscience, yet in thine own life, in thine own dealings with such ye show forth that love, that patience that He hast shown with the sons of men since He has called into being *bodies*—physically—that are known in the material world that these may furnish a channel through which those things that are known and accepted as being the qualifications of a spiritual life may *find* manifestations, and thus bring forth their fruits, their meats, ready for repentance.

For, while in humbleness of heart yet, in gladness does

each soul find those things, those loads to be met day by day. And as there is the step taken here and there in the meditations (for, as He has given, "As oft as ye ask in my name, *believing,* it shall be done unto you"), He is faithful in His promises; for, as He has given, "I will not leave thee comfortless, but ye shall be quickened—even as the spirit in thee makes thee alive, makes thee aware of the joys that are thine through the service that thou may render to thy fellow man, in justness, in mercy, in just being kind, just being gentle to those here, there, that have become and do become thy lot to be measured with." For, there are no such things as perchance, but the law of demand, the law of supply, the laws of love are ever, ever in thine own hands day by day. For, when there comes the needs that thou shouldst show forth thy love that has been shed on thee in thy activities in a material world, the opportunities that may be measured to thy fellow man are shown. For, as He has given, "Inasmuch as ye have done it unto the least of these, my little ones, ye have done it unto me."

Hence, in thy steps, be acquainted with the Lord. Seek, in thy secret places, that He knoweth thee aright. And there will come those answers as thou meditatest in thine inner self as to what, where and how thou shalt measure thy steps day by day. For, justice and mercy and peace and harmony are as His gifts to those that seek His face. He has given, "If ye love me, keep my commandments." His commandments are not grievous, neither do they deny thee any influence, any material things that will make for joy in thine own experience. Rather do the fruits of mercy, peace, justice and harmony make for such in thine own experience.

Hence, follow in the ways that are set before thee, knowing that He will call thee by name. And he that *He* names is redeemed in His sight. And there is nothing to fear save self. For, as has been given, "I am persuaded there is nothing in heaven, in earth, in principalities or in powers, that may separate the soul from the love of the Father save the waywardness, the indecisions, the unkindnesses that the self may inflict upon self or the fellow man."

Keep the way. Feed His sheep. Tend His lambs, those that are in thy way, those thou meetest day by day. Let thine own light so shine that they may know that thou walkest, that thou talkest, oft with thy God.

Ready for questions.

**Q-1.** *Is this entity one who may properly now pursue the higher and inner development of its soul and psychic forces?*

**A-1.** It is, as has been indicated. And in the development of the psychic forces, of the psychic influences and powers in the experience, enter into the Holy of holies, cleansing the mind, the body, in whatsoever way and manner as prepareth or bespeaketh to thee that thou mayest present thyself in body and mind as being CLEAN and ready for the acceptance of that the Lord, thy God, may give thee in the way of directions. As He has promised to be thy guide, as He has sent His Son into the earth to show thee the way, be satisfied with nothing less than those that He may guide. Let thy prayer ever be:

*Thy will, O God, be done in me as Thou seest I have need of, that I may be one with Thee—even as that I possessed with Thee before the world was.*

**Q-2.** *Are the mental and physical bodies of this entity at war with each other in such a manner as to retard its soul and psychic development at the moment and, if so, in what manner and how best to overcome such condition?*

**A-2.** As indicated from that just given, such is not the condition. The way to meet all such, as has been indicated through these sources, is to seek in the mental mind the answer to all questions that may be presented in the things that may be thy experiences day by day, and have the answer within self as thou prayest. Then lay this answer before the Throne of grace, or mercy itself, as thou would meditate within the chambers of thine own heart, and the answer will be within self as to the necessary step, the necessary things to perform to be rid of the warring of the flesh with the spirit. While each body, each soul, in the flesh is subject to the flesh, yet—as has been given of Him, "Though ye may be in the world, ye may not be *of* this world, if ye will but put your whole trust, your whole love, your whole life, in His keeping." He will not lead thee astray. He will guide, guard and direct thee, even as has been given, "He loveth every one and giveth his own life for those that will come to Him."

In the preparations, then, for these warrings within, as has been given, meet them step by step. That that is given thee put to use, for only in the use of that which is thine own may this grow, even as patience and mercy and love and endurance and tolerance. Putting them to use they become those bulwarks that prevent an interception from carnal forces or the spirits of an evil influence. For, these are helpless in *His* sight; for He is made Lord of all.

**Q-3.** *Has this entity yet karmic debts from previous life experiences to be met and paid off? If so, briefly, of what nature and how best to be met with most benefit to others?*

**A-3.** Karmic influences must ever be met, but He has prepared a way that He takes them upon Himself, and as ye trust in Him He shows thee the way to meet the hindrances or conditions that would disturb thee in any phase of thine experience. For, karmic forces are: What is meted must be met. If they are met in Him that is the Maker, the Creator of all that exists in manifestation, as He has promised, then not in *blind* faith is it met—but by the deeds and the thoughts and the acts of the body, that through Him the conditions may be met day by day. Thus has He bought every soul that would trust in Him. For, since the foundations of the world He has paved the ways, here and there entering into the experience of man's existence that He may know every temptation that might beset man in all of his ways. Then in that as the Christ He came into the earth, fulfilling then that which makes Him that channel, that we making ourselves a channel through Him may—with the boldness of the Son—approach the Throne of mercy and grace and pardon, and know that all that has been done is washed away in that He has suffered that *we* have meted to our brother in the change that is wrought in our lives, through the manner we act toward him.

**Q-4.** *Has this entity yet karmic debts from previous life experiences to be met and paid off in regard to his immediate family? If so, briefly, of what nature and how best to be met with most benefit to them?*

**A-4.** No karmic debts from other sojourns or experiences enter in the present that may not be taken away in that, "Lord, have Thy ways with me. Use me as Thou seest fit that I may be one with Thee."

**Q-5.** *In the previous experiences given for this entity, his experiences seem to have been mostly in the economic fields. Why, then, has his present urge always been to express self through some form of art?*

**A-5.** Art and its higher meanings are meeting the economic influences in man in his every experience. That is easily seen by this entity, as it studies for the moment as to how that he has visualized God's glory in the earth and that man uses in his daily needs is but an expression of how those economic forces in the needs of the body of the man are blessed in their whole sense or terms.

Hence as the expression of this art in the soul of self to give expression to these very influences of nature itself that are the closest manifestations of the love of a merciful Father to a wayward son, it shows to the entity in his studies that these are but the expressions that may in their measures be meted to man in such a way and manner as may make him aware of the love of the Father. Not so much the obligation that man is to a merciful Father, but rather the privilege of the man in the presence of a merciful Father. Rather as the love of the man to the fellow man in the presence of Him who gives mercy and peace and life in all its phases in the experience of man, that he may but come to know His ways the better.

**Q-6.** *Had this entity any previous experiences on this earth during the Italian Renaissance period, or during the Roman period, and if so, briefly, in what periods and for what purpose?*

**A-6.** In both of these periods we find the activities of the entity, rather in the one in the expression of the physical forces of the body—in the Roman period—as in the gladiator's activity; while in the Renaissance we find rather the expression of self in—yes, some of the oils—Reese (?)—Reese (?) is a portion of that assigned—in one of the caves—now it's on a wall in—on a wall in a cave. These expressions were to give, as it were, the combination of all the periods into one.

For the moment turn thy mind, my brother, to what has been meant in the variations of manifestations in the flesh, and in the spirit or in the soul body in its sojourn in the environs of other spheres—where there are the manifestations, as has oft been pointed out, of one particular activity; that is, one enters for a specific activity in Mars, Mercury or Venus, and in Saturn for that cleansing that must come to all that have departed from the earth and have not kept the ways clean. But in the earth we find *all* rolled into one, with a body and a body-mind for self-expression.

Hence, as has been given in regard to the appearances and their associations with the economic forces and influences in the experiences of a people, so has the influence in the present brought to thine experience the necessities of the activities in these directions; yet that may be expressed in this material plane, this earth's activity, by self in those visualizations, in those activities in the material things, in the meeting of the things in the daily activities of life, that may find expression in *all* of those things that may be found throughout the spheres. For, as has been given by Him, "Other sheep I have that are not of this fold," for they were on their journey that they, too, might come and hear His voice, from His children and His brethren that would make known His ways. What, ye ask again, are His ways? Just being kind, just being patient, just that as He gave, "A new commandment I give unto you, that ye love one another, that ye love thy neighbor as thyself, that *thou* would stand in thy neighbor's stead. Not . . . everyone that saith Lord, Lord, shall be called, but he that doeth the will of the Father." So in thine judgments, in the associations, he that doeth the will—or seeks to know the will, He may thy ways guide, He may thy acts manifested in His experience bring to the soul the knowledge of thy walks with thy God. Hence, as has been said, when thou prayest, let thy meditation be: "Use me, O God, as thou seest I may better serve Thee; in my waking moments, in my walks and my dealings with my fellow man, be Thou the guide."

We are through.                                      442-3

# MEDITATION

## by Herbert Bruce Puryear, Ph.D.

## Part I

As we seriously consider the promise of "face to face may they speak with the Father and with the Son," (254-68) let us allow our consciousness to be expansive enough to sense the magnitude of such a statement. Consider this excerpt from Edgar Cayce reading 281-28:

> . . . make thy mind, thy body, as a fit subject for a visit of thy Lord, thy God. Then as ye seek *ye know*, as He hath given, that the wedding feast is prepared and thou hast bid the guests, and that ye have come with the garments of the feast with thy Lord, thy Master, thy King, thy Savior.
>
> For lowly as He was in His earthly ministry, He honored all such that gathered for the commemoration of a union of body, a union of mind, a union of strength for their worship, their sacrifice, their meeting with their God.
>
> So do ye in thy meditation. For thy prayer is as a supplication or a plea to thy superior; yet thy meditation is that thou art meeting on *common ground!*
>
> Then prepare thyself!

To help us perceive this phrase as the amazing invitation it truly is, let us paraphrase it again in invitational form.

> *My dear children:*
>
> *The Lord thy God invites thee to a wedding feast that has been prepared. It is His wish to honor all such that would gather for the commemoration of a union of body, a union of mind, a union of strength for their worship, their sacrifice, their meeting face to face with me on common ground.*
>
> *Please dress appropriately with the garments of the feast.*
>
> *Eternally,*
>
> *Your Father*
>
> *RSVP*

Of the many ways in which this meeting face to face may be expressed or articulated, one says that we meet Him in the temple of our bodies; another suggests that we may experience the face-to-face meeting simply in the form of our prayers directed to the Divine. However, none makes it more clear than the above reading in its differentiation between prayer as a supplication to a superior and meditation as meeting on *common* ground.

Meditation, then, becomes for us not only one of the greatest opportunities on earth, but the greater opportunity of any dimension. With the raising of consciousness in meditation we may not only meet God face to face but stand with Him on common ground, *holy ground.*

Perhaps one of the most beautiful and important of all of them, reading 281-13, was given for a group that had gathered about Mr. Cayce in 1931 to conduct a work of prayer and healing.\*About a year after this first Prayer Group formed, the members asked for a specific discourse on meditation and prayer. Here is what they were told.

First, to "analyze that difference . . . between meditation and prayer." Prayer is defined as "the *making* of one's conscious self more in attune with the spiritual forces that may manifest in a material world, and is *ordinarly* given as a *cooperative* experience of *many* individuals . . ." With this comment we are immediately warned not to be as Pharisees who wished to be seen and who made their long prayers to be heard by men. We are warned that prayer should not be the pouring out of personality for outward show. Rather we are to pray in the spirit of entering into the closet of one's inner self and pouring out *self* so that we may be filled with the spirit of the Father.

Meditation, then, is defined as "prayer, but is prayer from *within* the *inner* self, and partakes not only of the physical inner man but the soul that is aroused by the spirit of man from within." If prayer is "the *making* of one's conscious self more in attune with the spiritual forces," then meditation seems to involve a portion of ourselves which is deeper than the conscious. It is an internal, physiological process and it involves the arousal of the soul.

\*The 131 readings given to the original Study Group have been published in Volume 7 of the Edgar Cayce Library Series, entitled *The Study Group Readings.* The 65 readings given to the Glad Helpers Prayer Group are contained in Volume 2 of the same series under the title, *Meditation: Part I.*

Now this physiological consideration is a problem for many. We know that the body is involved in and responsive to many forms of experience—to music, food, athletic activity, dancing, dramatic productions, aromas, television shows. Yet in the face of this well-accepted, well-established, personally experienced knowledge, we may be resistant to the notion that the body is involved in the attunement process of meditation. The readings affirm that "there are *definite* conditions that arise . . . A physical condition happens, a physical activity takes place! Acting through what?" We are now about to be introduced to a teaching which for some is bewildering and confusing; and yet it is one of the most important insights that we may gain as souls incarnate in the earth plane—how the one force of God meets, comes in contact with, influences, presents itself face to face with our physical consciousness.

The readings describe points of contact between the infinite spirit of God and the finite body of a person in terms of "the *imaginative* or the *impulsive* . . . sources." When we shut out thoughts pertaining to carnal forces, there may be aroused within us a response in the seat of the soul's dwelling.

The expression, "the imaginative forces," appears frequently in the readings, is of great importance, and needs to be studied thoroughly. The quality of mind as the builder is an aspect of soul, an aspect of the Father in us, His children. When this creative quality of mind as builder is expressed in the imaginative forces, the body responds, and impulses within the body are associated with such thoughts. We must not confuse the mind, but with the intellect or just the conscious mind, but with deeper processes which physiologically are more closely associated with the autonomic nervous system than with the sensory system.

How is this deeper nervous system aroused by the mind? Imagine expressions such as "There's a fire in the next room!" or "That's the best movie I have ever seen; you really must see it" or "I love you." In each of these expressions a quality may be given in the spirit and tone of the voice such that we either believe them or we do not, we find them credible or not, we are emotionally aroused and stimulated by them or not. That *quality* that makes them come alive for us and creates a different emotion or response in action is the same quality that is here referred to as the imaginative or the impulsive forces.

**If there has been set the mark (mark meaning here the image that is raised by the individual in its imaginative and impulse force) such that it takes the form of the ideal the individual is holding as its standard to be raised to, within the individual as well as to all forces and powers that are magnified or to be magnified in the world from without, _then_ the individual (or the image) bears the mark of the Lamb, or the Christ, or the Holy One, or the Son, or any of the names we may have given to that which _enables_ the individual to enter THROUGH IT into the very presence of that which is the creative force from within itself—see?**

Imprinted and patterned on the mind of the soul is a model of the Divine. In the psychology of Carl Jung this might be called an archetype of the Self. This pattern of the integrated uniqueness of the individual may be quickened by the imaginative forces of the mind when the motivation behind it, or the ideal, is in accord with it. Now we have been instructed that the most important experience for any individual is to know what is the _ideal_ spiritually. (The _ideal_ refers to the criterion of motivation which we have set; the motivational qualities of intent, purpose, desire, indeed the _spirit in which_ we do whatever we do.)

If the most important experience for any individual is to know the spiritual ideal, then what is being shared here with respect to meditation and the meeting of God on common ground is of the utmost importance. If our ideal bears the mark of the Divine within, then we also may be said to bear the mark (and notice the inclusiveness of this promise) "of the Lamb, or the Christ, or the Holy One, or the Son, or (observe again) any of the names we may have given to that which _enables_ the individual to enter THROUGH IT into the very presence of" God.

The reading says, "any of the names," putting aside the limitations of language and dogma. In the same sentence, we are told of something "which _enables_ (us) to enter THROUGH IT" to the presence of God. Now many would have us believe, because we are immersed in the spirit of God and He is all about us, that we may immediately turn to Him and in our own consciousness be in His presence. The query, sometimes the complaint, is "Am I not already there?" Why do I need something or someone *through which* to enter into that?"

The truth of the human condition is that we have built thought forms, desire patterns, and thus physiological response systems that tend to keep us cut off from an awareness of our oneness with God. And there are many levels of the subconscious and spirit planes that intrude. When we turn within, we are confronted with these patterns of our own making and the thought forms of others, which constitute barriers to our awareness of the oneness with God. However, a *way*, a *pattern* has been prepared by which we may pass through these limitations into the true heritage of the soul as a child of God.

Now we are warned in the reading more specifically that some have so abused the mental attributes of the body as to make scars, so that only an imperfect image may be raised. Such a person meditating has a great and challenging work ahead to begin to get a sense of God's love and forgiveness. His desire for at-onement with Him may inspire an ideal, a quickening imagery to the imaginative forces of the mind. Indeed the Christ, our Friend and Mediator, will quicken and inspire the response of the soul to a new sense of promise and hope and grace. "Some have so overshadowed themselves by abuses of the mental attributes of the body as to make scars, rather than the mark, so that only an imperfect image may be raised . . ."

The expression, "abuses of the mental attributes," is a warning regarding the kind of mental imagery upon which we may dwell, our mental food, which may interfere with the imaginative forces when the meditator seeks to raise the forces in meditation. All previous arguments pro and con about various moralities and behaviors are relative in the face of such considerations. The question is not whether it's right or wrong to do something; now it's a question of the way in which a mental attribute may, through the imaginative forces, make for hindrances to raising the life force itself to bring about the higher consciousness of the soul. This is a new criterion for self-inventory.

And yet we are assured that, even if we have fallen short, from these centers within the body there may arise the very essence of life itself and that these functions never reach a point at which they cease to secrete that which makes for the vital forces within the body. Specific centers are mentioned in this context: the lyden and gonads, which relate to the creative and sexual or reproductive centers at the base of the spine; the pineal, which is at the base of the brain; and the pituitary, referred to here as "the hidden eye in the center of the brain system . . ." The lyden and pineal together make that which, from the point of view of the readings, constitutes the very seat of the soul itself in the physical body! And the pituitary, the master gland of the body, is the coordinating center for all of the forces in the body from which may be disseminated the life force for the healing of self and others.

How, then, in meditation may this life force be raised in attunement to this highest center from which it may be disseminated? In an understatement, frequently characteristic of the readings, a perennial truth is revealed: "It has been found throughout the ages (*individuals* have found) that self-preparation (to *them*) is necessary." Here seems to be an awareness that all deeply experienced meditators know to be true and many beginning meditators feel unnecessary for themselves—the preparation in terms of the individual himself. And so the warning:

> So, to *all* there may be given:
> *Find* that which is to *yourself* the more certain way to your consciousness of *purifying* body and mind, before ye attempt to enter into the meditation as to raise the image of that through which ye are seeking to know the will or the activity of the Creative Forces; for ye are *raising* in meditation actual *creation* taking place within the inner self!

We are to find *for ourselves* the more certain way to our own consciousness of the proper preparation and purification.

The expression, "actual *creation* taking place within the inner self," suggests that the one force, the spiritual energy in meditation, is actually brought into manifestation in material form in the physical body. Later in the reading we are told that meditation "properly done must make one *stronger* mentally, physically, for has it not been given (that) He went in the strength of that meat received for many days?" Even the Master had need of entering into the silence to gain sustenance; and as we follow His pattern and enter "with a clean hand, a clean body, a clean mind, we may receive that strength and power that fits (us) for a greater activity in this material world."

Some very specific steps are given for preparation and cleansing and the reasons for them. Some people have claimed to have been meditating according to Edgar Cayce's method for years and yet receiving little in the way of experiences or confirmation. However, these same persons may admit to not doing some of the preparatory steps which the readings indicate are so helpful and important: the specific breathing procedures to normalize the respiratory and the circulatory systems, the use of odors or incense not only to stimulate spiritual awareness but also to aid in laying aside carnal or material influences. As the body is purified, "the purity of thought as it rises has less to work against in the dissemination of that it brings to the whole of the system, in its rising through the whole of these centers . . ."

Further suggestions are given: incantations or chanting, the drone of certain sounds, "the tolling of certain tones, bells, cymbals, drums or various kinds of skins." We are warned that we, "as higher thought individuals," may find fault with the way in which savages use these methods. Nevertheless, through these same principles there may "be raised . . . a *cleansing* of the body."

We each are invited again to find the more certain way for ourselves. When we find that which cleanses—whether it relates to food or interpersonal associations, activities of thought—then we may experience the forces raised and the healing of every kind "may be disseminated on the wings of thought . . ."

In the opening suggestion, the group asked for instructions that would enable them to "meditate, or pray, without the effort disturbing the mental or physical body." Now we are assured that "when one has cleansed self, in whatever manner it may be, there may be no fear that it will become so overpowering that it will cause any physical or mental disorder. It is *without* the cleansing that entering into such finds *any* type or any form of disaster, or of pain, or of any dis-ease of any nature."

Thus, for a second and a third time the meditator is warned about the importance of preparation and purification. "Cleanse the body with pure water. Sit or lie in an easy position . . ." A specific breathing procedure is given. Low music or the incantation of a chant is recommended. The imaginative forces are required for seeing, feeling, experiencing the image in the creative forces of love and entering into the Holy of holies.

Then as the raising of this energy occurs, we are instructed to see it disseminated through the inner eye through which we may be able to meet every condition in the experience of the body.

Again, the reading differentiates between prayer and meditation. "Prayer is the concerted effort of the physical consciousness to become attuned to the consciousness of the Creator . . . *Meditation* is *emptying* self of all that hinders the creative forces from rising along the natural channels of the physical man to be disseminated through those centers . . ."

A final warning and promise: "Be not afraid, it is I." If that which we raise in the inner self is the image of the Christ, love of the God consciousness, this in and of itself makes the body so cleansed as to be barred against all powers that would in any manner hinder. "Be thou CLEAN, in Him."

Finally, appended to reading 281-13 in the A.R.E. Library files is a most beautiful and appropriate letter of Edgar Cayce written to a friend. Apparently the friend had experienced a personal awareness of the Master and was questioning it, and so Mr. Cayce wrote:

> *Often I have felt, seen and heard the Master at hand. Just a few days ago I had an experience which I have not even told the folk here. As you say, they are too scary to tell, and we wonder at ourselves when we attempt to put them into words, whether we are to believe our own ears, or if others feel we are exaggerating or drawing on our imagination; but to us indeed they are often that which we feel if we hadn't experienced we could not have gone on.*
>
> *The past week I have been quite "out of the running," but Wednesday afternoon when going into my little office or den for the 4:45 meditation, as I knelt by my couch I had the following experience: First a light gradually filled the room with a golden*

*glow, then seemed to be very exhilarating, putting me in a buoyant state. I felt as if I were being given a healing. Then, as I was about to give the credit to members of our own group (281) who meet at this hour for meditation (as I felt each and every one of them were praying for and with me), HE came. He stood before me for a few minutes in all the glory that He must have appeared in to the three on the Mount. Like yourself I heard the voice of my Jesus say, "Come unto me and rest."*

Such experiences invite us once again to claim as a personal promise: "face to face, may they speak with the Father and with the Son." (254-68)

# Reading Number 281-13 _____

*This psychic reading given by Edgar Cayce at his home on Arctic Crescent, Virginia Beach, Va., November 19, 1932, in accordance with request made by Edgar Cayce himself.*

*Mrs. Cayce: You will have before you the psychic work of Edgar Cayce, present in this room, the information that has been and is being given from time to time, especially that regarding meditation and prayer. You will give, in a clear, concise understandable manner just how an individual may meditate, or pray, without the effort disturbing the mental or physical body. If this can be given in a general manner, outline it for us. If it is necessary to be outlined for specific individuals, you will tell us how individuals may attain to the understanding necessary for such experiences not to be detrimental to them.*

Mr. Cayce: Yes, we have the work, the information that has been and that may be given from time to time; especially that in reference to meditation and prayer.

First, in considering such, it would be well to analyze that difference (that is not always understood) between meditation and prayer.

As it has been defined or given in an illustrated manner by the Great Teacher, prayer is the *making* of one's conscious self more in attune with the spiritual forces that may manifest in a material world, and is *ordinarily* given as a *cooperative* experience of *many* individuals when all are asked to come in one accord and one mind; or, as was illustrated by:

Be not as the Pharisees, who live to be seen of men, who make long dissertation or prayer to be heard of men. They *immediately* have their reward in the physical-mental mind.

Be rather as he that entered the temple and not so much as lifting his eyes, smote his breast and said, "God be merciful to me a sinner!"

Which man was justified, this man or he that stood to be seen of men and thanked God he was not as other men, that he paid his tithes, that he did the services required in the temple, that he stood in awe of no one, he was not even as this heathen who in an uncouth manner, not with washed hands, not with shaven face attempted to reach the throne of grace?

Here we have drawn for us a comparison in prayer: that which may be the pouring out of the personality of the individual, or a group who enter in for the purpose of either outward show to be seen of men; or that enter in even as in the closet of one's inner self and pours out self that the inner man may be filled with the spirit of the Father in His merciful kindness to men.

Now draw the comparisons for meditation: Meditation, then, is prayer, but is prayer from *within* the *inner* self, and partakes not only of the physical inner man but the soul that is aroused by the spirit of man from within.

Well, that we consider this from *individual* interpretation, as well as from group interpretation; or individual meditation and group meditation.

As has been given, there are *definite* conditions that arise from within the inner man when an individual enters into true or deep meditation. A physical condition happens, a physical activity takes place! Acting through what? Through that man has chosen to call the imaginative or the impulsive, and the sources of impulse are aroused by the shutting out of thought pertaining to activities or attributes of the carnal forces of man. That is true whether we are considering it from the group standpoint or the individual. Then, changes naturally take place when there is the arousing of that stimuli(us) *within* the individual that has within it the seat of the soul's dwelling, within the individual body of the entity or man, and then this partakes of the individuality rather than the personality.

If there has been set the mark (mark meaning here the image that is raised by the individual in its imaginative and impulse force) such that it takes the form of the ideal the individual is holding as its standard to be raised to, within the individual as well as to all forces and powers that are magnified or to be magnified in the world from without, *then* the individual (or the image) bears the mark of the Lamb, or the Christ, or the Holy One, or the Son, or any of the names we may have given to that which *enables* the individual to enter THROUGH IT into the very presence of that which is the creative force from within itself—see?

Some have so overshadowed themselves by abuses of the mental attributes of the body as to make scars, rather than the mark, so that only an imperfect image may be raised within themselves that may rise no higher than the arousing of the carnal desires within the individual body. We are speaking individually, of course; we haven't raised it to where it may be disseminated, for remember it rises from the glands known in the body as the lyden, or to the lyden (cells of Leydig) and through the reproductive forces themselves, which are the very essence of Life itself within an individual—see? for these functionings never reach that position or place that they do not continue to secrete that which makes for virility to an individual physical body. Now we are speaking of conditions from without and from within!

The spirit and the soul is within its encasement, or its temple within the body of the individual—see? With the arousing then of this image, it rises along that which is known as the Appian Way, or the pineal center, to the base of the *brain,* that it may be disseminated to those centers that give activity to the whole of the mental and physical being. It rises then to the hidden eye in the center of the brain system, or is felt in the forefront of the head, or in the place just above the real face—or bridge of nose, see?

Do not be confused by the terms that we are necessarily using to give the exact location of the activities of these conditions within the individuals, that we may make this clarified for individuals.

When an individual then enters into deep meditation:

It has been found throughout the ages (*individuals* have found) that self-preparation (to *them*) is necessary. To some it is necessary that the body be cleansed with pure water, that certain types of breathing are taken, that there may be an even balance in the whole of the respiratory system, that the circulation becomes normal in its flow through the body, that certain or definite odors produce those conditions (or are conducive to producing of conditions) that allay or stimulate the activity of portions of the system, that the more carnal or more material sources are laid aside, or the whole of the body is *purified* so that the purity of thought as it rises has less to work against in its dissemination of that it brings to the whole of the system, in its rising through the whole of these centers, stations or places along the body. To be sure, these are conducive, as are also certain incantations, as a drone of certain sounds, as the tolling of certain tones, bells, cymbals, drums, or various kinds of skins. Though we may as higher thought individuals find some fault with those called savages, they produce or arouse or bring within themselves—just as we have known, do know, that there may be raised through the battle-cry, there may be raised through the using of certain words or things, the passion or the thirst for destructive forces. Just the same may there be raised, not sedative to these but a *cleansing* of the body.

"Consecrate yourselves this day that ye may on the morrow present yourselves before the Lord that He may speak through *you!*" is not amiss. So, to *all* there may be given:

*Find* that which is to *yourself* the more certain way to your consciousness of *purifying* body and mind, before ye attempt to enter into the meditation as to raise the image of that through which ye are seeking to know the will or the activity of the Creative Forces; for ye are *raising* in meditation actual *creation* taking place within the inner self!

When one has found that which to self cleanses the body, whether from the keeping away from certain foods or from certain associations (either man or woman), or from those thoughts and activities that would hinder that which is to be

---

42

raised from *finding* its full measure of expression in the *inner* man (*inner* man, or inner individual, man or woman, meaning in this sense those radial senses from which, or centers from which all the physical organs, the mental organs, receive their stimuli for activity), we readily see how, then, *in* meditation (when one has so purified self) that *healing* of *every* kind and nature may be disseminated on the wings of thought, that are so much a thing—and so little considered by the tongue that speaks without taking into consideration what may be the end thereof!

Now, when one has cleansed self, in whatever manner it may be, there may be no fear that it will become so overpowering that it will cause any physical or mental disorder. It is *without* the cleansing that entering into such finds *any* type or any form of disaster, or of pain, or of any dis-ease of any nature. It is when the thoughts, then, or when the cleansings of *group* meditations are conflicting that such meditations call on the higher forces raised within self for manifestations and bring those conditions that either draw one closer to another or make for that which shadows (shatters?) much in the experiences of others; hence short group meditations with a *central* thought around some individual idea, or either in words, incantations, or by following the speech of one sincere in abilities, efforts or desires to raise a cooperative activity *in* the minds, would be the better.

Then, as one formula—not the only one, to be sure—for an individual that would enter into meditation for self, for others:

Cleanse the body with pure water. Sit or lie in an easy position, without binding garments about the body. Breathe in through the right nostril three times, and exhale through the mouth. Breathe in three times through the left nostril and exhale through the right. Then either with the aid of low music, or the incantating of that which carries self deeper—deeper—to the seeing, feeling, experiencing of that image in the creative forces of love, enter into the Holy of holies. As self feels or experiences the raising of this, see it disseminated through the *inner* eye (not the carnal eye) to that which will bring the greater understanding in meeting every condition in the experience of the body. Then listen to the music that is made as each center of thine own body responds to that new creative force that is being, and that is disseminated through its own channel; and we will find that little by little this entering in will enable self to renew all that is necessary—in Him.

First, *cleanse* the room; cleanse the body; cleanse the surroundings, in thought, in act! Approach not the inner man, or the inner self, with a grudge or an unkind thought held against *any* man! or do so to thine own undoing sooner or later!

Prayer and meditation:

Prayer is the concerted effort of the physical conscious-ness to become attuned to the consciousness of the Creator, either collectively or individually. *Meditation* is *emptying* self of all that hinders the creative forces from rising along the natural channels of the physical man to be disseminated through those centers and sources that create the activities of the physical, the mental, the spiritual man; properly done must make one *stronger* mentally, physically, for has it not been given He went in the strength of that meat received for many days? Was it not given by Him who has shown us the Way, "I have had meat that ye know not of?" As we give out, so does the *whole* of man—physically and mentally—become depleted, yet in entering into the silence, entering into the silence in meditation, with a clean hand, a clean body, a clean mind, we may receive that strength and power that fits each individual, each soul, for a greater activity in this material world.

"Be not afraid, it is I." Be sure it is Him we worship that we raise in our inner selves for the dissemination; for, as He gave, "Ye must eat of my *body;* ye must drink of *my* blood." Raising then in the inner self that image of the Christ, love of the God consciousness, is *making* the body so cleansed as to be barred against all powers that would in any manner hinder.

Be thou CLEAN, in Him.

We are through for the present.                    281-13

# Part II

That practice in the spiritual life beside which there is none other is meditating in the silence. Wherever spirituality lives, there are those who sit in the silence. Learning how to meditate is an endeavor with which everyone should be concerned. One day all of us must come to make this practice a portion of our lives. For those interested in becoming channels of healing for others, meditation is indispensable.

In 1931 a group gathered around Edgar Cayce to receive a series of readings for spiritual development. Out of that group came a smaller number who gathered for the purpose of a healing ministry to others. To this smaller group was given a series of readings including special instructions on meditation. Although the readings encouraged many people to meditate and gave instructions for its practice, there were also occasions on which specific discourses were given on this subject.

In 1932 this healing group was given a lengthy and beautiful discourse on meditation. (See reading 281-24 following "The Laws of Spiritual Healing.") Seven years later another full discourse was given on this subject. This later reading, 281-41, is a challenging and instructing summons to the practice of the silence. In our endeavor to claim the promise of the covenant that we may meet our God face to face, meditation is precisely the claiming of that promise.

Reading 281-41 begins with an assessment of how concerned we are about such matters as meditation. For some people it makes no difference. Others do not care. However, for those for whom life *must* hold a special something else, this information was given.

We find ourselves confused about life in the earth and its meaning, with bodies and minds "not all beautiful" and "not all clean." In this assessment the readings indicate our present status and our need for this practice. And then address the specific question, "What is meditation?"

It is "not musing, not daydreaming" as many may think. This suggests that sitting in the silence and musing or daydreaming is actually what we do most of the time and call meditation. Uninformed or poorly motivated practices of the silence are not true meditation.

The readings pick up on the triune theme to remind us that we are physical, mental and spiritual. Meditation is "the attuning of the mental body and the physical body to its spiritual source." The implication of this definition is that our three bodies are not always in attunement or in accord. The existence of a spiritual body or soul is denied by many; but this reading reminds us that the very fact that we hope, that we have a desire for better things, that we are able to be sorry or glad, indicates an activity of the mind that is not temporal in nature but is rather an indication of the nature of our very being, the soul.

This reminder that we are souls may be underestimated. We would do well to reflect upon qualities that do indicate to us something within that desires a relationship with the Infinite, with the Eternal. Our true being is that which was made in the image of God, the soul. Meditation "is the attuning of thy physical and mental attributes seeking to know the relationships to the Maker. *That* is true meditation."

Although this definition may be known and frequently reiterated, it is often neglected with respect to an indication of the clear requirements of the activities and processes that must be involved in the proper practice of the silence. We are reminded that we must *learn* to meditate. We learn to walk. We learn to talk. We learn many other activities. We must *learn* to meditate.

It is interesting that as the readings instruct us that we must learn to meditate that the examples given are not of some complex or difficult task or skill, but the most elementary experiences of childhood, learning to walk and to talk. These are skills which we have all learned. We consider these to be so basic to human experience that we hardly think of them as learning occasions except when we are in the presence of a child, observing the learning procedure in process. Imagine the number of times a child in trying to learn to walk pulls to a stand, falters, stumbles, and tries again and again. Or imagine the process of learning to talk. On the one hand, it is so difficult for us to learn a foreign language; however, it seems so natural to think of a child learning a language as we observe the step-by-step growth from the first words to the beautiful and articulate expressiveness of one who is only five or six years old.

Then we are instructed on the points of contact between these bodies that may enable that oneness or attunement to occur between the consciousness and that potential of every soul, the superconsciousness. We are warned not to let words set limitations on something which is as boundless as is the soul. Nevertheless an awareness is needed that there are physical contacts within the body, some not even discoverable by anatomists, which play the role of channels for the processes; and glands function as rallying points for the energies which are involved in and centrally relevant to meditation. Therefore, an understanding of the body and the function of these centers is of great importance to the proper practice of meditation. We are warned that these centers in many are dormant, in others atrophied, because of nonactivity or the diversion of the abilities into dissipative desires and activities. With this background we are given the first step in meditation:

". . . purify thy mind if ye would meditate." Purify the mind. How? This depends upon the individual's concept of purification. It is a matter of being true to the inner self to get a sense of what for yourself, as an individual, constitutes purifying. What would *you* do to prepare yourself to meet God face to face? There are discoverable principles regarding this. But the growth is in doing whatever for each individual seems to be indicated. Then each must act upon his or her own choices, not merely in terms of following instructions about how to meditate, but in actually doing that in the everyday life which works toward the purification of the mind.

A good way to consider this process is to observe what claims your attention when indeed you do sit down and try to enter the silence. Do you find that your mind goes quickly to a movie you have just seen or a television program or to a certain kind of music or to a relationship with another person? Does it move toward a project that you are looking forward to participating in? Then as we observe these tendencies, we begin to see some of the things held in the mind that work against attunement which would enhance the approach to the Divine. Purification necessitates our leaving off these experiences that detract from our attunement. Purifying of the mind takes place over time with a growing awareness of the subtleties of thought patterns and distractions.

This quest for the Divine now as always must be within the inner self. The body is the temple. It is within that He has promised to meet us. When we contemplate this promise, this possibility, this amazing and almost unthinkable confrontation with God within our own present limited being, we become doubtful, or perhaps afraid or ashamed. But this is the great invitation to every soul. Then let us set our house in order.

We are reminded of the points of physical contact in the body which relate it to the mind and the soul. Just as the prick of a needle is followed by an awareness of pain because there are activities in consciousness related to messages sent through the nervous system to the brain, in the same simple and straightforward manner there are contacts in the body with the soul.

We are asked, "What is thy God?" How essential it is that we be clear about this! As meditators, we need to understand the Divine, our relationship to Him, and the processes required to bring the physical and mental in attunement with that Reality.

In consideration of "What is thy God?" we are asked to take an inventory of our ambitions and aspirations. If we expand this question to ask how much of our time and consideration is given to the acquisition, management, and spending of material resources, we are on the right track to make an inventory of our desires. "What is our desire?" relates quite directly to "What is our God?" Is our God only to eat tomorrow or to fulfill concerns of how we may be clothed and what more we can have? For many of us this may be true far more than we are willing to admit.

We may not only re-examine but reorder our desires and motivations. We may begin to release desires and motivations of one kind in favor of mobilizing and energizing desires and motivations toward the Divine. If meditation is meeting God within our own bodies which are the temples given us as the means for such an approach, then the desire must be first to know Him. This is the essence of the meditative practice, that beside which there is no other which may assure our quick success. The desire first must be to know Him.

There is a story from the East of a guru walking with his student (or chela) who expressed to his teacher, "Master, I want to know God." The response of his teacher was to grab his student by the hair, drag him quickly into the nearby river and to hold his head under the water until he was sputtering, almost drowning. Then he raised his head up and said to him calmly, "When you want to know God as badly as you wanted that breath of air, you may begin to make some progress."

First, we need to desire to know Him. One way in which we may begin to put that desire into activity is by purging the body and the mind of those things we conceive of as being hindrances to that endeavor. This is not doing what someone else says. It is rather changing what in our *own* minds constitutes a hindrance to serious meditation. The Edgar Cayce readings frequently mention Biblical passages such as Deuteronomy 30, Jeremiah 31, Hebrews 10, and Romans 10, that indicate that "it isn't who will descend from heaven to bring you a message, nor who would come from over the seas, but lo, ye find Him within thine own heart, within thine own consciousness!"

As we study Biblical passages on the law which is written within our hearts and mouths so that we may know it and do it, let us remember that the law is the pattern within. As the Psalmist says, "Blessed is he who meditates day and night on the law of the Lord." (Psalm 1:1-2)

The second step is to purify the *body*. Involved in this is shutting ourselves away from the cares of the world. The implications of this are that the bodily processes are kept out of attunement when we concern ourselves with things of the world, such as worry, anger, appetites, and desires. Once again we are challenged as from the days of old to a consideration of the convenant the Father made with us so that we may meet Him face to face. And we are instructed, "Think on that as ye would do to have thy God meet thee face to face." We are warned that such a consideration may make us fearful. Have we gone so far astray that we cannot realize that an all-loving, all merciful, all-powerful Father-God would not only already know but also eagerly supply what is truly needed for the attuning of the physical and mental to our true being?

We are told, "Sanctify thy body, as the laws were given of old, for tomorrow the Lord would speak with thee . . ." It would be well for the serious student to review some of those Old Testament passages in which instructions for purification were outlined. These must be studied not fearfully or resentfully, but rather as a perspective; these are not given to discourage or to limit, but to help us discover what we may need. They may be helpful in bringing about the body's greater attunement to its spiritual source.

One of the books of the Old Testament in which these laws are most fully expressed is Leviticus. In studying this book, let us remember that the readings encourage us to carry out our own concept of what is the proper personal preparation. And whatever this may be, we need to be true to it. Make the choice and do it and not merely say it.

If we are fearful, we are reminded of the invitation of the Father, "If ye will be my children, I will be thy God" and "Though ye wander far away, if ye will but call I will hear." We may continue to question this, but the indication in these readings is that the heart of the meditative process is the direct approach to God. And so we are reminded again in a statement alluding to a passage in Hebrews 11:6 that

**They that would know God, would know their own souls, would know how to meditate or to talk with God, must believe that He *is*—and that He rewards those who seek to know and to do His biddings.**

These are the essentials: Purify the mind, purify the body, believe that God *is*. Although in this discourse faith in God may be outlined as the third step given, this may be the first, most important and always requisite step in meditation. Then let us be clear about this: Love of God is the commandment; love of God is the essence of meditation.

From the readings' point of view, meditation is essentially approaching the Divine within. It is purifying the physical and the mental so that there may be an attunement of the physical and mental to the spiritual body, the soul. The soul is that part of our true being which has the potential of superconsciousness, that is to say, the awareness of oneness with God. Then meditation is approaching God. The requirements in this approach are to purify the mind and purify the body, and of course the belief that God is and that in our endeavors to purify mind and body in our quest for Him, that He will reward our search.

> If there has been set the mark (mark meaning here the image that is raised by the individual in its imaginative and impulse force) such that it takes the form of the ideal the individual is holding as its standard to be raised to, within the individual as well as to all forces and powers that are magnified or to be magnified in the world from without, *then* the individual (or the image) bears the mark of the Lamb, or the Christ, or the Holy One, or the Son, or any of the names we may have given to that which *enables* the individual to enter THROUGH IT into the very presence of that which is the creative force from within itself . . . 281-13

This marvelous paragraph summarizes in so many ways how meditation awakens the pattern within which enables us to become wholly one with God.

Now we are given an additional step in learning how to meditate.

> . . . if ye will *meditate*, open thy heart, thy mind! Let thy body and mind be channels that *ye* may *do* the things ye ask God to do for you! Thus ye come to know Him.
>
> Would you ask God to do for you that you would not do for your brother?

We are warned that the practice of meditation requires changes in the activities of our daily lives. We *must* begin to do those things that we would inquire of the Divine. There must be a consistency between our practices in relationships with others and what we are asking God to do for us. Are we asking God to forgive us while we are still holding something against another? Thus the instructions for meditation seem to require an inventory of what needs to be done in our lives with respect to ourselves and others. Measuring up to our own ideals will enable us to attune the physical and mental to the spiritual. The essence of the meditating process is facilitated by activities in the daily life in which we see Him in others.

A tremendously beautiful, penetrating and promising challenge to approach the Divine is given in this:

> For He is not past finding out; and if ye will know Him, tune in to Him; turn, look, hope, act in such a way that ye *expect* Him, thy God, to meet thee face to face. "Be not afraid, it is I," saith He that came to

**those seeking to know their relationship with their Maker.**

Remember that challenge and admonition from the New Testament where we are invited to the mind of Christ? "Let this mind be in you which was also in Christ Jesus; who . . . thought it not robbery to be equal with God . . . And being found in fashion as a man, he humbled himself, and became obedient unto death . . ." (Philippians 2:5-8)

It may be that some will read this reading and go away saying, "I do not understand." There may be a sense that specific instructions on how to meditate have not been fully developed. However, the problem may be that we expect certain instructions for how to meditate when the steps that are given in this reading may be far more central to the issue than we imagine at first glance. Here, in fact, we may have been given the deepest and most significant instruction on what we need to know in learning the practice of the silence.

As we address this marvelous potential, we are warned again and again not to be afraid. Why are we afraid? Why do we still say, "I do not understand?" Why have we so belittled ourselves that we disqualify ourselves from that greatest and most important of all opportunities to have the consciousness of knowing our Maker? It is true that we must humble ourselves. However, humbling does not mean that we do not make the approach. And if we come with an open, seeking, contrite heart, desirous of having the way shown—and when we are shown do not turn our face the other way—then He will speak to us as He has promised. "When ye call I will hear, and will answer speedily."

If we could only find it in ourselves to take these simple and eternal promises seriously, to recognize ourselves as souls, children of the Most High, to get a sense of the Reality of His Being, the depth of His love, and the eager forgiveness of the Father for His children! If we could open ourselves to these straightforward truths of life, then we would find a tremendous joy in life. We would be deeply motivated to seek these moments of silence in meditation that so fully renew, refresh, and imbue life with hope and promise. And we would experience an ability to aid others such that our lives and theirs would be wondrously and gloriously changed.

Let us then find within ourselves a new commitment to

say as was given of old, "Others may do as they may, but as for me, I will worship—yea, I will serve the living God." And then we may be assured that

**He is not far from thee! He is closer than thy right hand. He standeth at the door of thy heart! Will ye bid him enter? or will ye turn away?**

# Reading Number 281-41 _____

*This psychic reading given by Edgar Cayce at the Hotel Warner . . . Avenue, Virginia Beach, Va., June 15, 1939 . . .*

*Mrs. Cayce: You will have before you those assembled here who seek information on meditation which will be helpful to them and others.*

Mr. Cayce: In the mind of many there is little or no difference between meditation and prayer. And there are many gathered here who, through their studies of various forms, have very definite ideas as to meditation and prayer.

There are others that care not whether there be such things as meditation, but depend upon someone else to do their thinking, or are satisfied to allow circumstance to take its course—and hope that some time, somewhere, conditions and circumstances will adjust themselves to such a way that the best that may be will be their lot.

Yet, to most of you, there must be something else—some desire, something that has prompted you in one manner or another to seek to be here now, that you may gather something from a word, from an act, that will either give thee hope or make thee better satisfied with thy present lot, or to *justify* thee in the course ye now pursue.

To each of you, then, we would give a word:

Ye all find yourselves confused at times respecting from whence ye came and whither ye goeth. Ye find yourselves with bodies, with minds—not all beautiful, not all clean, not all pure in thine own sight or in thy neighbor's. And there are many who care more for the outward appearance than that which prompts the heart in its activity or in its seeking.

But ye ask, what has this to do with meditation? What *is* meditation?

It is not musing, not daydreaming; but as ye find your bodies made up of the physical, mental and spiritual, it is the attuning of the mental body and the physical body to its spiritual source.

Many say that ye have no consciousness of having a soul—yet the very fact that ye hope, that ye have a desire for better things, the very fact that ye are able to be sorry or glad, indicates an activity of the mind that takes hold upon something that is not temporal in its nature—something that passeth not away with the last breath that is drawn but that takes hold upon the very sources of its beginning—the *soul*—that which was made in the image of thy Maker—not thy body, no—not thy mind, but thy *soul* was in the image of thy Creator.

Then, it is the attuning of thy physical and mental attributes seeking to know the relationships to the Maker. *That* is true meditation.

How do you accomplish same? How would ye as an individual go about learning to meditate?

For, ye must learn to meditate—just as ye have learned to walk, to talk, to do any of the physical attributes of thy mind as compared to the relationships with the facts, the attitudes, the conditions, the environs of thy daily surroundings.

Then, there must be a conscious contact with that which is a part of thy body-physical, thy body-mental, to thy soul-body or thy superconsciousness. The names indicate that ye have given it metes and bounds, while the soul is boundless—and is represented by many means or measures or manners in the expressions in the mind of each of you.

But there are physical contacts which the anatomist finds not, or those who would look for imaginations or the minds. Yet is is found that within the body there are channels, there are ducts, there are glands, there are activities that perform no one knows what! in a living, *moving*, thinking being. In many individuals such become dormant. Many have become atrophied. Why? Non-usage, non-activity! because only the desires of the appetite, self-indulgences and such, have so glossed over or used up the abilities in these directions that they become only wastes as it were in the spiritual life of an individual who has so abused or misused those abilities that have been given him for the greater activity.

Then, purify thy mind if ye would meditate. How? Depending on what is thy concept of purification! Does it mean to thee a mixing up with a lot of other things, or a setting aside of self, a washing with water, a cleansing or purifying by fire or whatnot?

Whatever thy concept is, be *true* to thine inner self. *Live* that choice ye make—*do it!* not merely say it but *do it!*

Purify thy body. Shut thyself away from the cares of the world. Think on that as ye would do to have thy God meet thee face to face. "Ah," ye say "but many are not able to speak to God!" Many, you say, are fearful. Why? Have ye gone so far astray that ye cannot approach Him who is all merciful? He knows thy desires and thy needs, and can only supply according to the purposes that ye would perform within thine own self.

Then, purify thy body, physically. Sanctify thy body, as the laws were given of old, for tomorrow the Lord would speak with thee—as a father speaketh to his children. Has God changed? Have ye wandered so far away? Know ye not that, as He has given, "If ye will be my children, I will be thy God"? and "Though ye wander far away, if ye will but call I will hear"?

If any of you say, "Yes, but it was spoken to those of old— we have no part in such," then indeed ye have no part. They that would know God, would know their own souls, would know how to meditate or to talk with God, must believe that He *is*—and that He rewards those who seek to know and to do His biddings.

That He gave of old is as new today as it was in the beginning of man's relationship or seeking to know the will of God, if ye will but call on Him *within* thine inner *self!* Know that thy body is the temple of the living God. *There* He has promised to meet thee!

Are ye afraid? Are ye ashamed? Have ye so belittled thy opportunities, have ye so defamed thine own body and thine own mind that ye are ashamed to have thy God meet thee within thine own tabernacle?

Then, woe be unto thee—lest ye set thy house in order. For as has been indicated, there are physical contacts in thy own body with thy own soul, thy own mind. Does anyone have to indicate to you that if you touch a needle there is pain felt? Ye are told that such an awareness is an activity of consciousness that passes along the nervous system to and from the brain. Then, just the same there are contacts with that which is eternal within thy physical body. For there is the bowl that must one day be broken, the cord that must one day be severed from thine own physical body—and to be absent from the body is to be present with God.

What is thy God? Are thy ambitions only set in whether ye shall eat tomorrow, or as to wherewithal ye shall be clothed? Ye of little faith, ye of little hope, that allow such to become the paramount issues in thine own consciousness! Know ye not that ye are His? For ye are of His making! He hath willed that ye shall not perish, but hath left it with thee as to whether ye become even aware of thy relationships with Him or not. In thine own house, in thine own body there are the means for the approach—through the desire first to know Him; putting that desire into activity by purging the body, the mind of those things that ye know or even conceive of as being hindrances—not what someone else says! It isn't what you want someone else to give! As Moses gave of old, it isn't who will descend from heaven to bring you a message, nor who would come from over the seas, but lo, ye find Him within thine own heart, within thine own consciousness! if ye will *meditate*, open thy heart, thy mind! Let thy body and mind be channels that *ye* may *do* the things ye ask God to do for you! Thus ye come to know Him.

Would you ask God to do for you that you would not do for your brother? If you would, you are selfish—and know not God. For as ye do it unto the least of thy brethren, ye do it unto thy Maker. These are not mere words—they are that as ye will *experience*—if ye would know Him at all. For He is not past finding out; and if ye will know Him, tune in to Him; turn, look, hope, act in such a way that ye *expect* Him, thy God, to meet thee face to face. "Be not afraid, it is I," saith He that came to those seeking to know their relationship with their Maker. And because He came walking in the night, in the darkness, even upon the waters, they were afraid. Yea, many of you become afraid because of the things that ye hear—for ye say, "I do not *understand*—I do not *comprehend!*" Why? Have ye so belittled thyself, thy body, thy mind, thy consciousness, that thou hast seared, that thou hast made of none effect those opportunities within thine own consciousness to know thy Maker?

Then, to all of you:

Purify thy body, thy mind. Consecrate thyselves in prayer, yes—but not as he that prayed, "I thank Thee I am not like other fellows." Rather let there be in thy heart that humbleness, for ye must humble thyself if ye would know Him; and come with an open, seeking, contrite heart, desirous of having the way shown to thee.

And when thou art shown, turn not thy face the other way; but be true to the vision that is given thee. And He will speak, for His promise has been, "When ye call I will hear, and will answer speedily." Then, when He speaks, open thy heart, thy mind to the opportunities, to the glories that are thine—if ye will but accept them through that attuning through meditation of thy consciousness, thy desire to the *living* God; and say and live within thyself as he of old gave, "Others may do as they may, but as for me, I will worship—yea, I will serve the living God."

He is not far from thee! He is closer than thy right hand. He standeth at the door of thy heart! Will ye bid Him enter? or will ye turn away?

281-41

# THE WHEEL OF THE LAW

## by Violet M. Shelley

Reincarnation, when it first appeared in one of Edgar Cayce's readings in 1925, brought both consternation and confusion to Cayce and those around him. Cayce, whose psychic gift had been misused in the past, was concerned that evil forces had taken over his talent. Those around him, who were just as unfamiliar with the concept as he, were at a loss to know how this alien idea would fit within the familiar framework of the Christ-oriented Cayce readings. Further study and many questions were finally to convince them all that there was nothing inherent in the concept of reincarnation which could be construed as inconsistent with, or contradictory to, Christianity.

However, after the first fears were allayed and acceptance replaced skepticism, the attitude of that early group changed to one of fascination with past lives and associations, a response both natural and common to many people when first considering the possibility of having lived before. Subsequent readings, such as 5731-1, given in June, 1933, were instrumental in changing the focus from one of fascination to the realization of the awesome responsibility that the concept implied for the soul, the self.

Reincarnation, also called *the continuity of life,* is a way of explaining the immortality of the soul. It has been said that one neither hears of it nor considers it at all until one is ready. The readings indicate that once we have understood and accepted the belief we can never again turn our backs on it and its attendant implications without serious penalty. The concept of reincarnation postulates that the soul has lived before and will live again and again until it has been perfected by making its will one with that of its Creator.

This reading speaks of the reality of the soul:

**A soul, an entity, is as real as a physical entity, and is as subject to laws as the physical body is subject to the laws in a material world and the elements thereof!**

Elsewhere in the Cayce material are statements that we do not *possess* souls, we *are* souls. This is something that we tend to overlook as we, in our self-concern, continue to think of our reality as being minds, bodies, and personalities—and those unique and alone. It has often been said that although we are never confused between a man and his overcoat, or a man and the car he is driving, we are forever confusing the reality of the man with the body that he's in!

The laws to which souls, as very real entities, are subject are universal and immutable, and the process of reincarnation is a number of these laws at work. These laws operate with the same consistency as do the laws that apply to manifestations in the material world. Like those laws—the law of gravity, for example—they continue to operate whether one believes in them or not!

Reincarnation suggests that it is a combination of such laws that requires souls to return to the earth in a varied succession of appearances. Cayce was asked to address the reason for this in the 1933 reading. Included was the explanation that it was not the Father's choice, rather it was the souls themselves who had made these trips necessary.

**Each soul that enters, then, must have had an impetus from some beginning that is of the Creative Energy, or of a first cause.**

**What, then, was—or is—the first cause; for if there be law pertaining to the first cause it must be an unchangeable law, and is—*is*—as "I AM that I am! For this is the basis from which one would reason:**

**The first cause was, that the created would be the companion for the Creator; that it, the creature, would—through its manifestations in the activity of that given unto the creature—show itself to be not only worthy of, but companionable to the Creator.**

And that's how the whole cycle of reincarnation began. Souls were created to be companions to God and given the opportunity to demonstrate their worthiness through their activities. They were endowed with free will:

**Then a soul, the offspring of a Creator, entering into a consciousness that became a manifestation in any plane or sphere of activity, given that free will for**

**its use of those abilities, qualities, conditions in its experience, demonstrates, manifests, shows forth, that it reflects in its activity towards that first cause.**

The gift of free will was part of the Creator's plan, for without it souls could never have become true companions and co-creators; they would be no more than automatons. They were intended to use the gift to demonstrate in their expressions and experiences the Divine Spirit of which they were a part. Other readings in the Cayce files elaborate more on this, saying that souls used their wills and creative abilities to project themselves into the material plane, where through their own desires, they got stuck. It is the law of reincarnation that provides the way for them to work their way out of that dimension.

Perhaps the reason the parable of the prodigal son has such a poignant appeal for so many of us is because we realize at some level of our being that it is *our* story. It is we who, as souls, have taken our inheritance, free will, from the Father, and have squandered it in a far country. Entrapped in the earth by our earthly desires and choices, we finally yearn for something better. We feel a longing to get back to our lost estate, to take the least of positions just to be there.

The poignancy of the parable is in the promise it holds forth; for the Father saw his son coming from a long way off and went out to meet him. The same welcome awaits us, for when we decide to start the journey home, help is immediately at hand. Thus, this reading states, if we are to understand ourselves we need to be aware of whence we came.

If our souls are part of the Divine Spirit and the Divine Mind, why are we not more aware of our origin and heritage? Noel Langley in his book on reincarnation* compared the experience of a soul in the earth to a diver's experience under water. He describes the day on the deck as bright and clear, and the sea appearing smooth and transparent. The diver dons an old-fashioned diving suit, lead-weighted boots and heavy copper helmet. He is then lowered into the water to investigate a long-submerged wreck. Memory of the clear day above the water fades as the diver with limited vision has to struggle against the currents in the dark and murky water of the seabed. Reality stops being life on the deck of the ship

*Edgar Cayce on Reincarnation, Hawthorn Books, New York, N.Y., 1967.

and starts being a battle of survival accompanied by the struggle to remember the charts and the plans that had seemed so simple before his descent. When the diver is finally hauled back into the sunshine, the memory of what seemed interminable hours below gradually becomes a vague dream, and reality is once again life on the ship and the security there.

As the prodigal son had to decide to start home, so does the diver have the lifeline of oxygen connecting him to the ship. He needs only to use it to signal for help from above. A similar lifeline is available to us in prayer and meditation.

Both prodigal son and diver left both comfort and security by choice, and we, as souls, are in the material plane by choice. We are here because we wanted to be gods all by ourselves, but it didn't work.

**What caused the first influences in the earth that brought selfishness? The desire to be as gods, in that rebellion became the order of the mental forces in the soul; and sin entered.**

In this rebellion, souls, considering themselves to be separate from the Divine Mind of which they were a part, created by this identification their self-conscious minds. The feeling of separation continues as long as we identify with this very small portion of the mind. The self-conscious mind acts as a barrier to the superconscious part of the mind, the Divine within. Every selfish thought, word, or act makes that barrier harder to penetrate and widens the gulf. But separation is an illusion, and the barrier built by us can also be torn down by us. It is the self-conscious mind we learn to bypass in meditation. We begin to chip away at it when we give ourselves in service, when we think of others rather than ourselves.

Man in the earth is a triune being consisting of *body, mind,* and *soul,* and in the earth is subject to all the laws of the material plane. But the readings tell us that life is continuous and 5753-1 goes on to state that in whatever sphere of consciousness the soul manifests, it is always subject to the laws of that plane, and there, as well as here, must learn to demonstrate its desire to bring its will into at-oneness with that of the Creator. The purpose of the soul discarnate is still the same, for mind and will are still present.

**Because an atom, a matter, a form, is changed, does not mean that the essence, the source or the spirit of it has changed; only its form of manifestation, and *not* in its relation with the first cause.**

No urge is stronger than that of the will, and any gains the soul ever makes in efforts to align its will with the Creator remain forever a part of the soul's individuality. We are told here that the soul's consciousness is not lost between lives.

Readers who are familiar with the life readings given by Edgar Cayce (those which describe past incarnations and their influence on the present life of an individual) will remember that in the beginning of each one were references to planets which were affecting the life. Over the years there have been many attempts to correlate these references with modern astrology, but so far nothing definitive has been published. More to the point is to look at the readings themselves for clarification. They indicate that between its lives in the earth, the soul exists in mental dimensions, and planets were used to symbolize these dimensions. What a person did with and dwelt on in an incarnation determined the sphere to which the soul would go at the end of the life. Nor would that necessarily be the last stop before another life. Learning could continue and progression made to still other dimensions, and this was always dependent on what the soul did with its consciousness and its will. The planets named at the start of the life reading represented the mental dimension where the soul had been most recently and indicated the mental predisposition the soul brought into the current experience.

The aura chart readings which were given for some of the people who had had life readings stressed that an individual's mental bent was the result of time between lives in the earth, and that the emotional nature had been built by past lives in the earth.

Reading 5753-1, discussing this aspect of the law of reincarnation, asserts that it is an example of the Law of Attraction at work.

**Like begets like. Those things that are positive and negative forces combine to form in a different source, or different manifestation, the combinations of which each element, each first principle manifested, has gained from its associations—in its activities—**

**that which has been brought to bear by self or that about it, to produce that manifestation.**

**Hence man, the crowning of all manifestations in a material world—a causation world, finds self as the cause and the product of that he (man), with those abilities given, has been able to produce, or demonstrate, or manifest from that he (the soul) has gained, does gain, in the transition, the change, the going toward that (and being of that) from which he came.**

Thus, we find that we have not entered on the cycle of reincarnation and are not bound by the laws pertaining to it as a result of the original divine plan. We, ourselves, are both the *cause* and the *effect*—as the reading says, the *product.* Every effort we make toward returning whence we came remains a part of the soul, and the opportunity to exercise our wills toward this end is available in whatever dimension we find ourselves.

That the Law of Attraction determined where our time is spent between lives was reaffirmed in the answer to the third question at the end of this reading:

**Hence the entity develops *through* the varied spheres of the earth and its solar system, and the companions of varied experiences in that solar system, or spheres of development or activity; as in some ways accredited correctly to the planetary influences in an experience. The entity develops through those varied spheres.**

**Hence the sun, the moon, the stars, the position in the heavens or in all of the hosts of the solar systems that the earth occupies—all have their influence in the same manner (this is a very crude illustration, but very demonstrative) that the effect of a large amount of any element would attract a compass. Drawn to! Why? Because of the influence of which the mind element of a soul, an entity, has become conscious!**

This Law of Attraction, expressed in *Like begets like* and *We reap what we sow,* is often referred to as *karma.* This word has, in my opinion, become something of a maligned and misunderstood term, mostly associated only with its negative aspects. Too often it is regarded as retribution for some forgotten action in the dim and misty past. Such a view makes its holder feel like an innocent victim, much like a child punished for a misdeed of three weeks ago.

We need to remember that *Like begets like* works as well one way as the other; therefore, our good deeds and thoughts attract those of similar nature. We need to realize that we justly deserve the good and loving things that happen to us, for we are reaping what we have sown. To understand karma, the positive aspect must be stressed as much as the negative.

And how negative is the negative aspect? Perhaps it is only a question of attitude toward it. Rather than punishment, it is possible that it is only another face of grace. Our higher selves are patient teachers and put before us lessons, again and again, until we have mastered them. Some of the readings call it "meeting self," and an apt phase it is, for as we meet what we have built we have the opportunity to forgive and to be forgiven, and as we do, our souls become more worthy of their rightful place.

Some years ago I found myself in a situation to which I felt tied, and I proceeded to pronounce it *karmic*. Someone older and wiser told me that if it was karmic, then I would indeed be tied to it until I learned to love it! It was the best advice, for, when I changed my attitude, the burden seemed to disappear magically. Today it's hard to remember that I ever felt the situation was so onerous.

Further, this reading emphasizes that when the soul finds that it must work out its own salvation by entering and re-entering the material world, the Law of Forgiveness is in effect. The Christ is the Way and is ever ready to aid the soul in its becoming one with the Father.

We are the cause and the product. We got the cycle of incarnating started and through our choices we have kept it going. How, then, do we reverse the process? One of the most important keys appears repeatedly in the Cayce readings in the statement, "Thoughts are things." Concomitant is the enjoinder, at times only implied, that we must learn to control our thoughts. No longer can we content ourselves with ethical and moral outward behavior and consider our thoughts to be both private and inconsequential. We must control our thoughts because what we dwell on mentally we become or draw to us. Worry is the dwelling on dire things that might happen and has been dubbed *negative prayer*; as Job said, "What I feared has come upon me." The Law of Attraction applies to our thoughts. That those thoughts are deeply etched is illustrated vividly by an instance when in the midst of giving a reading Cayce commented that the person's past lives were difficult to define because it was almost impossible to discern the difference between what he thought and what he did.

All of our thoughts are being recorded on that ceaseless tape recorder referred to in the readings as "the skein of time and space." Are they worthy of being there, or are most of them involved with petty self-concerns? Only we can control our thoughts; and learn to control them we must, for they were the building blocks of our past lives and our present life, and they are the stuff of which our future is made.

> **Just as it is when an entity, a body, fills its mind (mentally, materially) with those experiences that bespeak of those things which add to the carnal forces of an experience. Just so does the mind become the builder throughout. And the mental mind, or physical mind, becomes carnally directed!**
> **The mind is the builder ever, whether in the spirit or in the flesh. If one's mind is filled with those things that bespeak of the spirit, that one becomes spiritual-minded . . . Choose ye . . .**

It is one thing to acknowledge that our free will is our inheritance, our birthright, and quite another thing to realize that we use or abuse this gift constantly in the choices that we make. The choice of thought, attitude, action, and speech is present every waking moment. The decision is ours as to whether those choices will make us the worthy companions of the Creator we were meant to be.

"As a man's desire is, so is his destiny. For as his desire is, so is his will; and as his will is, so is his deed; as his deed is, so is his reward, whether good or bad . . ." (*Brihadarayaka Upanishad*)

Choice plays a major role in controlling our thoughts. As the readng indicates, we can choose to dwell on the material or the spiritual, the negative or the positive. There are times when the only choice open to us is one of attitude. When the readings talk about turning "stumbling blocks into stepping-stones," it is this choice of attitude to which they refer.

Daily quiet times for prayer and meditation help us learn to control our thoughts and to change our attitudes. Using the affirmation in *A Search for God*, Book I, helps us to align our wills with that of the Father.

*Not my will but Thine, O Lord, be done in me and through me. Let me ever be a channel of blessings, today, now, to those I contact in every way. Let my going in, my coming out be in accord with that Thou would have me do, and as the call comes, "Here am I, send me, use me!" ("Cooperation")*

Meditation is the lifeline to the kingdom of heaven which is within each one of us; and regular meditation helps us break through the illusory barrier of the self-conscious mind into the bright world of Spirit.

Earlier, I mentioned that when first accepting the concept of reincarnation people often tend to become bemused by romanticizing past lives. Others begin to wonder how long the cycle needs to go on. One man asked Cayce how long he would need to keep reincarnating, and the answer was, "How long will you require?" Implicit in that answer is all the loving patience and eternal forgivenss of the Father.

Some 1200 individuals had life readings by Edgar Cayce, and in 18 of those the information was volunteered that, providing those people kept in the way they were going, they might have the choice of not returning to earth again. Evidently when bound to the Wheel of the Law, such a choice is not readily available. Wondering if there was a common denominator in these lives, I studied them in detail for the A.R.E. Press book, *Reincarnation Unnecessary* (Virginia Beach: A.R.E. Press, 1979). Thinking that perhaps they had all led lives that would qualify them for sainthood, I found instead that they were just average people, from all walks of life, struggling with a variety of problems. What they had in comon, however, was selflessness. They were all *giving* people, giving self to others, giving more than receiving, giving to the development of others in every plane. We are reminded of the Master's teaching that we possess only what we give away. One of the individuals was told that he had truly shown that he put his brother first. Other comments from that group of readings appropriate here are that only as an individual gives in service does he or she become aware; and another is the reminder that the conquering of self is greater than the conquering of many worlds.

These readings demonstrate the truth set out in 5753-1:

Until we apply the teachings of Jesus and make them a part of our soul's individuality, we will not be in a position to choose whether or not to return to the earth. These cases offer evidence that such a position is not impossible to attain. The choice is before us daily.

> . . . heaven and hell (are) built by the soul! The companionship in God is being one with Him; and the gift of God is being conscious of being one with Him, yet apart from Him—or one with, yet apart from the Whole.

The accompanying Cayce reading on reincarnation testifies to the loving justice of our Creator and assures us that the kingdom of the Father has been prepared for us from the foundation of the world. We are today in the best place possible to start our homeward journey by letting our wills become one with our Creator's. The only thing that can ever stand in the way is *self*. We are the cause and we are the product.

# Reading Number 5753-1 ____

*This psychic reading was given by Edgar Cayce at his home, on the 16th day of June, 1933, before the Second Annual Congress of the Association for Research and Enlightenment, Inc., in accordance with request by those present.*

*Mrs. Cayce: You will give at this time a comprehensive discourse on reincarnation. If the soul returns to the earth through a succession of appearances, you will explain why this is necessary or desirable and will clarify through explanation the laws governing such returns. You will answer the questions which will be asked on this subject.*

Mr. Cayce: Yes. In giving even an approach to the subject sought here, it is well that there be given some things that may be accepted as standards from which conclusions—or where parallels—may be drawn, that there may be gathered in the minds of those who would approach same some understanding, some concrete examples, that may be applied in their own individual experience.

Each soul that enters, then, must have had an impetus from some beginning that is of the Creative Energy, or of a first cause.

What, then, was—or is—the first cause; for if there be law pertaining to the first cause it must be an unchangeable law, and is—*is*—as "I AM that I am!" For this is the basis from which one would reason:

The first cause was, that the created would be the companion for the Creator; that it, the creature, would—through its manifestations in the activity of that given unto the creature—show itself to be not only worthy of, but companionable to, the Creator.

Hence, every form of life that man sees in a material world is an essence or manifestation of the Creator; not the Creator, but a manifestation of a first cause—and in its own sphere, its own consciousness of its activity in that plane or sphere.

Hence, as man in this material world passes through, there are the manifestations of the attributes that the consciousness attributes to, or finds coinciding with, that activity which is manifested; hence becomes then as the very principle of the law that would govern an entrance into a manifestation.

Then a soul, the offspring of a Creator, entering into a consciousness that became a manifestation in any plane or sphere of activity, given that free will for its use of those abilities, qualities, conditions in its experience, demonstrates, manifests, shows forth, that it reflects in its activity towards that first cause.

Hence in the various spheres that man sees (that are demonstrated, manifested, in and before self) even in a material world, all forces, all activities, are a manifestation. Then, that which would be the companionable, the at-oneness with, the ability to be one with, becomes necessary for the demonstration or manifestation of those attributes in and through all force, all demonstration, in a sphere.

Because an atom, a matter, a form, is changed, does not mean that the essence, the source or the spirit of it has changed; only in its form of manifestation, and *not* in its relation with the first cause. That man reaches that consciousness in the material plane of being aware of what he does about or with the consciousness of the knowledge, the intelligence, the first cause, makes or produces that which is known as the entering into the first cause, principles, basis, or the essence, that there may be demonstrated in that manifested that which gains for the soul, for the entity, that which would make the soul an acceptable companion to the Creative Force, Creative Influence. See?

As to how, where, when and what produces the entrance into a material manifestation of an entity, a soul:

In the beginning was that which set in motion that which is seen in manifested form with the laws governing same. The inability of destroying matter, the ability of each force, each source of power or contact—as it meets in its various forms, produces that which is a manifestation in a particular sphere. This may be seen in those elements used in the various manifested ways of preparing for man, in many ways, those things that bespeak of the laws that govern man's relationship to the first cause, or God.

Then, this is the principle:

Like begets like. Those things that are positive and negative forces combine to form in a different source, or different manifestation, the combinations of which each element, each first principle manifested, has gained from its associations—in its activities—that which has been brought to bear by self or that about it, to produce that manifestation.

Hence man, the crowning of all manifestations in a material world—a causation world, finds self as the cause and the product of that he (man), with those abilities given, has been able to produce, or demonstrate, or manifest from that he (the soul) has gained, does gain, in the transition, the change, the going toward that (and being of that) from which he came.

Periods, times, places: That which is builded, each in its place, each in its time.

This is shown to man in the elemental world about him. Man's consciousness of that about him is gained through that he, man, does about the knowledge of that he is, as in relation to that from which he came and towards which he is going.

Hence, in man's analysis and understanding of himself, it is as well to know from whence he came as to know whither he is going.

Ready for questions.

**Q-1.** *What is meant by inequality of experience? Is it a strong argument for reincarnation?*

**A-1.** Considering that which has just been presented, isn't it the same argument?

**Q-2.** *Is experience limited to this earth plane?*

**A-2.** As each entity, each soul, in the various consciousnesses, passes from one to another, it—the soul—becomes conscious of that about self in that sphere to which it, the entity, the soul attains in a materially manifested way or manner.

Hence the entity develops *through* the varied spheres of the earth and its solar system, and the companions of varied experiences in that solar system, or spheres of development or activity; as in some ways accredited correctly to the planetary influences in an experience. The entity develops through those varied spheres.

Hence the sun, the moon, the stars, the position in the heavens or in all of the hosts of the solar systems that the earth occupies—all have their influence in the same manner (this is a very crude illustration, but very demonstrative) that the effect of a large amount of any element would attract a compass. Drawn to! Why? Because of the influence of which the mind element of a soul, an entity, has become conscious!

A soul, an entity, is as real as a physical entity, and is as subject to laws as the physical body is subject to the laws in a material world and the elements thereof!

Does fire burn the soul or the physical body?

Yet, self may cast self into a fire element by doing that the soul knows to be wrong!

What would make a wrong and a right? A comparison of that the soul knows its consciousness to be in accord or contrariwise with, in relation to that which gave it existence.

**Q-3.** *Are not transferred memories misappropriated by individuals and considered to be personal experiences?*

**A-3.** Personal experiences have their influence upon the inner soul, while disincarnate entities (that may be earthbound, or that may be heaven-bound) may influence the thought of an entity or a mind.

But, who gives the law to have an element to influence, whether from self or from another? That same as from the beginning. The will of the soul that it may be one with the first cause.

In the material, the mental, the spiritual experience of many souls, many entities, it has been found that there *be* those influences that *do* have their effect upon the thought of those who would do this or that. Who gives it? Self!

Just as it is when an entity, a body, fills its mind (mentally, materially) with those experiences that bespeak of those things which add to the carnal forces of an experience. Just so does the mind become the builder throughout. And the mental mind, or physical mind, becomes carnally directed!

The mind is the builder ever, whether in the spirit or in the flesh. If one's mind is filled with those things that bespeak of the spirit, that one becomes spiritual-minded.

As we may find in a material world: Envy, strife, selfishness, greediness, avarice, are the children of *man*! Long-suffering, kindness, brotherly love, good deeds, are the children of the spirit of light.

Choose ye (as it has ever been given) whom ye will serve.

This is not (begging) the question! As individuals become abased, or possessed, are their thoughts guided by those in the borderland? Certainly! If allowed to be!

But he that looks within is higher, for the spirit knoweth the Spirit of its Maker—and the children of same are as given. And, "My Spirit beareth witness with thy spirit," saith He who giveth life!

What *is* Life? A manifestation of the first cause—God!

**Q-4.** *Explain, in the light of reincarnation, the cycle of development towards maturity in individuals.*

**A-4.** As an individual in any experience, in any period, uses that of which it (the soul or entity) is conscious in relation to the laws of the Creative Force, so does that soul, that entity, develop towards—what? A companionship with the creative influence!

Hence karma, to those disobeying—by making for self that which would be as the towers of Babel, or as the city of Gomorrah, or as the fleshpots of Egypt, or as the caring for those influences in the experience that satisfy or gratify self without thought of the effect upon that which it has in its own relation to the first cause! Hence to many this becomes as the stumbling block.

It is as was given by Him, "I am the way. No man approaches the Father but by me." But, does a soul crucify the flesh even as He, when it finds within itself that it must work out its own salvation in a material world, by entering and re-entering that there may be made manifest that consciousness in the soul that would make it a companion with the Creator?

Rather is the law of forgiveness made of effect in thine experience, through Him that would stand in thy stead; for He is the way, that light ever ready to aid when there is the call upon—and the trust of the soul in—that first cause!

Has it not been given that there *is* an influence in the mind, the thought of man, from the outside? Then, would those who have lost their way become the guides and both fall in the ditch? or would the soul trust in the Way, and the Light, and seek in that way that there may be shown the light?

What caused the first influences in the earth that brought selfishness? The desire to be as gods, in that rebellion became the order of the mental forces in the soul; and sin entered.

**Q-5.** *What is the strongest argument against reincarnation?*

**A-5.** That there is the law of cause and effect in *material* things. But the strongest argument against reincarnation is also, turned over, the strongest argument for it; as in *any* principle, when reduced to its essence. For the *law* is set— and it happens! though a soul may will itself *never* to reincarnate, but must burn and burn and burn—or suffer and suffer and suffer! For, the heaven and hell is built by the soul! The companionship in God is being one with Him; and the gift of God is being conscious of being one with Him, yet apart from Him—or one with, yet apart from the Whole.

**Q-6.** *What is the strongest argument for reincarnation?*

**A-6.** Just as given. Just turn it over; or, as we have outlined. We are through for the present.

5753-1

# THE LAWS OF SPIRITUAL HEALING

*by Herbert Bruce Puryear, Ph.D.*

Dis-ease and the desire for healing are universal. In every time and culture there have been stories and legends of those who could heal and of those who were healed by extraordinary means.

In our own time and culture this phenomenon is most frequently referred to as "faith healing." No one seems to deny that healing of this kind does occur. However, specific cases are regularly explained away as emotionalism, hypnosis, autosuggestion, "just" the imagination, spontaneous remission, or the placebo effect. Thus, with a few words, one of the most valuable and beautiful of all human experiences in the earth is dismissed.

These phenomena of healing occur in the face of those whose world view is said to be "scientific." This scientific world view implies that there is lawfulness underlying all phenomena. Yet, in spite of the solid evidence in support of the occurrence of such phenomena, those who espouse an objective approach tend to be both unwilling to look at the facts and unwilling to acknowledge that there may be laws underlying them which can, and indeed need to be, discovered and understood.

We are not concerned here with others' viewpoints but rather with our own. We students of the Edgar Cayce readings need more clarity of understanding and more commitment to the application of insights derived from such great promise of healing. What is important, then, is that we not allow the viewpoints of others, of self-appointed or culturally appointed authority—whether they be physicians, scientists, or ministers—or the viewpoint of the culture as a whole to discourage or dissuade us from moving to a deeper understanding and a new readiness for the application of these extraordinary laws.

There is spiritual healing. There is physical, mental, and emotional healing of a great array of disorders, some of which are termed incurable. These expressions of healing occur outside the applications of contemporary medicine or other modalities of healing ordinarily accepted in our present social structure. More than half a century ago, Edgar Cayce was giving information on the laws that underlie these phenomena.

Let us imagine this group of several people gathered around Edgar Cayce for reading 281-24 on the 29th of June, 1935. As members of this group asked for a discourse on the laws of spiritual healing, they must have been quite amazed, perhaps perplexed, by what turned out to be a discourse on atomic and subatomic physics. From this discourse we see that the points of contact between the non-manifest spirit and the manifest materiality are at the subatomic level.

In the beginning the reading mentions a corollary of the first premise of the oneness of all force found in the metaphysical principle relating the macrocosm to the microcosm. Man is made in the image of God. A single atom has within its structure the whole form of the universe: as above, so below.

With this imagery of the atom as a miniature solar system, we can envision the vital necessity of all these forces remaining in their proper orbs and balance for there to be harmony and soundness in the solar system. Thus it is with each individual atom. We can see how catastrophic it would be for the solar system were that balance not maintained.

Apparently it is possible for there to be a loss of such balance and equilibrium in the atom. When such is extended on a considerable scale within the physical body it is as catastrophic for the individual as for the solar system. If the atomic forces are not in proper equilibrium, then disease may result. This may come about, as indicated in the reading, from "an overbalancing, an injury, a happening, an accident . . ." wherein certain atomic forces may be destroyed or others increased.

The key, then, to physical health is the proper balance of the rotary forces of every atom within the body. A requirement for healing is the re-creation of that balance so that the atomic centers may have the proper equilibrium in their rotary forces. This is accompanied in the body by resuscitation and revivification. We are told that "it becomes necessary for the creating of that influence within each individual body to bring a balance necessary for its continued activity about each of the atomic centers its own rotary or creative force . . ."

Now let us think in terms of physics, of energy fields, instead of biology. Let us imagine a force field that has balance, equilibrium, and coherence. In these terms an excellent analogy may be seen in the phenomenon of magnetism. If a magnet is held near a nail, for example, the nail will become magnetized. What changes have taken place? None chemically, only an alignment, as it were, of the atomic and molecular forces within the nail.

This analogy may be applied almost literally to an understanding of the way that one person who has "so attuned or raised its own vibrations sufficiently . . . may—by the motion of the spoken word—awaken the activity of the emotions to such an extent as to revivify, resuscitate or to change the rotary force or influence or the atomic forces in the activity of the structural portion, or the *vital* forces of a body, in such a way and manner as to set it again in motion."

In such a process what enables the healer "to set it again in motion"? The reading earlier points out that it is "the motivative force of spiritual activity . . ." This means the flow of energy from the non-manifest into the manifest *for a right purpose*. Remember, our basic premise is the oneness of all force, that one force is spirit and that materiality as we know it is a projection of that force. The physics of this may be as simple or as complicated as Einstein's formula $E = mc^2$. We know that modern physics has already acknowledged that *matter* per se does not exist at the subatomic level, but that all is *energy*. And we know from scientific laboratory experiments that energy may be projected even at great distances, as in telepathy. In some experiments the thoughts of the healer have been shown to work over hundreds of miles to influence the activity of a cloud chamber in a physics laboratory.

The readings indicate that in meditation actual *creation* is taking place. We may interpret this as a movement from the level of pure energy into physical manifestation. This is a key to understanding healing.

The principle of healing is the same. It may be from another's attunement in prayer at a distance or in the laying on of hands or as a matter of fact (so the reading indicates) "by a look, by the application of any mechanical influence or any of those forces in *materia medica* . . ."

Let's inquire further as to what enables this to happen. We are told, "The law, then, is compliance with the universal spiritual influence . . ." So we may say that there are laws and that, with compliance with these laws, healing may naturally follow.

We have stressed the physics of this process. Let us now examine the biology of it. The reading indicates that "where another body may raise that necessary influence in the hormone of the circulatory forces as to take from that within itself to revivify or resuscitate diseased, disordered or distressed conditions within a body." The use of the term *hormone* reminds us of what we have learned about the relationships of the endocrine system to the spiritual centers within the body.

The seven spiritual centers of the body are like *senses.* Just as the eye is so constructed as to be sensitive to the energies of light, and the ear is so constructed as to be sensitive to the energies of sound, so these seven centers are sensitive to the subtle kinds of energy that may be projected by thoughts, as in mental telepathy or prayer.

We may again by analogy come to an understanding of this process if we liken it to a battery-operated radio. Just as the subtle energies of the radiowave may vibrate along the antenna and be amplified by the battery-supplied energy, so may the subtle energies of a thought or a prayer be picked up and amplified by the bodily energies of the recipient.

The antenna effect would be the entering of the thoughts through the spiritual centers into the subatomic levels of the endocrine glands. Here the input is translated into hormonal secretions which act as powerful messengers to order or reorder every cell of the body, bringing about the revivifying, resuscitation, or healing of the disordered condition.

Within every body exists a pattern for perfect functioning. Attuned energies can quicken those patterns, just as a tuning fork when struck causes reverberations in another tuning fork of the same frequency. When the spirit of life, light, and love is quickened in one person, it may be projected by thought or prayer to quicken a spirit of life, light, and love in another. The points of contact are the spiritual centers which, in turn, translate the input into hormonal messages of life, light, and love and carry them to all the forces of the body. With these messages the rotary forces about the atoms of every cell are quickened and restored to proper equilibrium.

These laws are not especially difficult to understand nor overly demanding in their fulfillment. Therefore, there should be a growing expectation on our part, indeed a new joy and zeal, in the understanding of these laws and the expectation for healing within ourselves and others.

What, then, sets these laws of healing in motion? The reading ends by making this clear: "It is in any manner the result only of compliance to the First Cause, and the activity of same within the individual's *relative* relation to its own evolution."

Let us especially notice "the result only of compliance to the First Cause . . ." What is compliance to the First Cause? These readings indicate that the whole answer for the world is that all must have the one ideal of the great commandment: to love God with all our hearts, minds, and souls and our neighbor as ourselves. Then compliance to the First Cause is the aligning of ourselves with the love of God. As we think of God not only as *love* but also as *law*, then we must begin to apply ourselves both to the spirit of love and to the laws of how the universe and ourselves are structured. It is clear that as we begin to be more loving and to act more in accord with what we know to be the law, we may expect to receive more healing in our own lives and to aid in bringing it into the lives of others.

Now other spiritual laws may be introduced to enhance this process. One of these is indicated in the answer to the first question in reading 281-24, that group action can be more effective than individual activity because where "there is oneness of purpose, oneness of desire" a synergistic effect gives greater enhancement than when individuals work separately or not in accord. This again is compliance with the First Cause, because the whole idea of love implies the necessity for oneness of purpose and oneness of desire. When these are found between two or more individuals, the flow of the energy of love is naturally enhanced.

There were those present for the reading who had a background in psychical research and so they raised questions related to the etheric body. The reading indicates clearly that there may on occasion be *possession* by discarnates, and it goes on to specify some conditions under which this may occur. One way in which there may come the possessive influences is "through pressure upon some portion of the anatomical structure that would make for the disengaging of the natural flow of the mental body through the physical . . ."

To understand possession we are reminded that there is the physical body, the mental body, and the soul body. Where incoordinations occur between the mental body and the physical body in relation to the soul influence, one may truly be "dispossessed of the mind; thus ye say rightly he is 'out of his mind.' " The disengaging of the natural flow of the mental body to the physical body is related also to a condition frequently referred to in the readings as the incoordination of the nervous systems. These pressures leading to incoordinations may be either structural or functional in origin, or both.

Examples of structural pressures are seen in instances of spinal subluxations for which osteophathic or chiropractic manipulation, or occasionally massage, is the recommended therapy. We can easily visualize how a structural pressure caused by a spinal subluxation might imbalance the rotary forces of the atoms in the affected tissues.

Other pressures may be brought about by dietary incoordinations, by problems of attitudes and emotions, or by an array of other disorders.

Let us take an example of the emotions. In the third answer we are told, "The mind, through anger, may make the body do that which is contrary to the better influences of same; it may make for a change in its environ, its surrounding, contrary to the laws of environment or hereditary forces that are a portion of the *élan vital* of each manifested body . . ."

Earlier in the reading we are told that the imbalancing of the atomic forces might include the destroying of some of these forces or the increasing of others. We can see how in anger some of the rotary forces about the atom might be increased in such a way as to work against the flow of the energy from the spirit level into the atomic forces.

Anger may produce a blockage of the flow of energy at the atomic level which may make for the incoordination of the nervous systems and thus leave the individual vulnerable to possessive influences. Where these imbalances or pressures specifically involve the endocrine glands, the special problem exists of the derangement of the spiritual sensory system and consequently the increased likelihood of possession.

A very important and serious consideration must be addressed as we encourage the meeting of God face to face within the temples of our own bodies. As our society becomes more interested in and acceptive of the reality of a world beyond the physical and as spiritual influences come into manifestation more in the lives of individuals, there will likely be greater potential for misunderstanding of the associated pathologies. "Such, then, become possessed as of hearing voices, because of their closeness to the border-land. Many of these are termed deranged when they may have more of a closeness to the universal than one who may be standing nearby and commenting; yet they are awry when it comes to being normally balanced or healthy for their activity in a material world."

With the opening of more and more individuals to the spirit plane or the borderland through a search for the inner life—whether through dreams, experiences in meditation, or a greater awareness of inner voices—those who open themselves but have not prepared themselves to deal with such energy in a balanced way may find themselves in serious trouble. Physical, mental and spiritual incoordinations may express through spinal subluxations, mental attitudes, karmic backgrounds, openness without discernment to the multitude of voices that may speak from the spirit plane.

One form of this imbalance which is most serious is in the case of the individual who may feel a special calling, even a sense of identity with the Christ. The individual may wonder about being an incarnation of Jesus and thus may feel that the forces are asking him to be the Second Coming of the Christ.

Of course, within us all abides the archetypal pattern of the Christ. When that is fully energized, we have the pattern for the manifestation of perfection. However, when this archetypal pattern is triggered or activated out of accord with the full, holistic attunement of the individual—in his ability to apply and live in that spirit—then comes the imbalance. We must recognize that we are children of God, each bearing the pattern of the Christ within, and that this pattern can and may—indeed *should*—become activated. However, there is also the individual development in time and space to be considered, as indicated in this reading— the factors of environment, heredity, and soul development upon which this influence may be imposed. So such experiences may confuse individuals, leading to an imbalancing of their experiences in consciousness.

It is true that, as the real spirit of the Christ begins to speak through us, changes are required of us, including new commitments, even "sacrifices." It is also true that a great work must be done in the earth and many of us need to rise to the challenge of that work, including the challenge of being channels through which the spirit may express. It is also true, however, that we must always prepare ourselves before, during, and after awareness of these experiences, so that we may continually purify and attune our channel through which this spirit may express. As we grow to be more fully attuned and balanced, manifestations of the spirit are given expression in terms of greater peace and joy to the individual, not in anxiety or confusion in the life. "By their fruits ye shall know them."

All of us then, as we align ourselves with the ideals and information of this work, need to begin to put our lives in order physically, mentally, and spiritually with a new zeal. As we pursue the attunement that may be gained in meditation, we will find that the spirit within will have a healthy and balanced channel through which to express. Thus may we manifest not only the gifts but also the fruits of the spirit in kindness, patience, long-suffering and brotherly love.

Question four is especially important and instructive.

Here the group asked ". . . how an individual may raise his own vibrations . . . to effect a self-cure." We are assured that this is possible by "raising that attunement of self to the spirit within, that is of the soul body . . ." How? "As the body-physical is purified, as the mental body is made wholly at-one with purification or purity, with the life and light within itself, healing comes, strength comes, power comes."

Two steps then are given: (1) purification of the physical body and (2) making the mental body at-one with purification or purity. This may be accomplished through meditation, but it is pointed out that the attunement must be complete or whole, not just partial. We are reminded of the physics of this. In meditation, actual *creation* is taking place: The spirit moves through space and time and comes into material expression.

The answer for healing becomes very simple: "Then *making* self in an at-onement with that Creative Force brings what? That necessary for the activity which has been set in motion and has become manifested to be in accord *with* that First Cause." What are these conditions?

**. . . it becomes necessary that ye speak, ye act, that way. For whosoever cometh to offer to self, or to make an offering to the Throne of mercy or grace, and speaketh unkind of his brother, is only partially awake or aware.**

Thus we see that the simple laws of all healing are that healing comes from the One Spirit, the life force, and that, as we put ourselves in accord with this First Cause, we may expect healing. Attuning self through meditation needs to be coupled with manifesting that attunement in application. This application is not in the doing of any great deed but simply in manifesting the fruits of the spirit: kindness, patience, long-suffering, brotherly love. Thus are we healed, made whole. Thus is our neighbor, our world, healed, made whole, made one.

# Reading Number 281-24 ___

*This psychic reading given by Edgar Cayce at his home*

on Arctic Crescent, Virginia Beach, Va., this 29th day of June, 1935, in accordance with request made by those present; second reading of the Association Fourth Annual Congress . . .

Mrs. Cayce: You will have before you the laws of spiritual healing. You will give a discourse at this time on psychic (spiritual) healing, describing just what takes place in the body and mind of one healed. You will answer the questions that may be presented.

Mr. Cayce: Yes, we have the laws that govern spiritual or psychic healing. Much has been given through these channels from time to time respecting that necessary in the individual experience for healing.

As we have indicated, the body-physical is an atomic structure subject to the laws of its environment, its heredity, its *soul* development.

The activity of healing, then, is to create or make a balance in the necessary units of the influence or force that is set in motion as the body in the material form, through the motivative force of spiritual activity, sets in motion.

It is seen that each atom, each corpuscle, has within same the whole form of the universe—within its *own* structure.

As for the *physical* body, this is made up of the elements of the various natures that keep same in its motion necessary for sustaining its equilibrium; as begun from its (the individual body's) first cause.

If in the atomic forces there becomes an overbalancing, an injury, a happening, an accident, there are certain atomic forces destroyed or others increased; that to the physical body become either such as to add to or take from the *élan vital* that makes for the motivative forces through that particular or individual activity.

Then, in meeting these it becomes necessary for the creating of that influence within each individual body to bring a balance necessary for its continued activity about each of the atomic centers its own rotary or creative force, its own elements for the ability of resuscitating, revivifying, such influence or force in the body.

How, then, does the activity of *any* influence act upon the individual system for bringing *healing* in the wake or the consciousness, to become conscious of its desire?

When a body, separate from that one ill, then, has so attuned or raised its own vibrations sufficiently, it may—by the motion of the spoken word—awaken the activity of the emotions to such an extent as to revivify, resuscitate or to change the rotary force or influence or the atomic forces in the activity of the structural portion, or the *vital* forces of a body, in such a way and manner as to set it again in motion.

Thus does spiritual or psychic influence of body upon body bring healing to any individual; where another body may raise that necessary influence in the hormone of the circulatory forces as to take from that within itself to revivify or resuscitate diseased, disordered or distressed conditions within a body.

For, as has been said oft, any manner in which healing comes—whether by the laying on of hands, prayer, by a look, by the application of any mechanical influence or any of those forces in *materia medica*—must be of such a nature as to produce that necessary within those forces about the atomic centers of a given body for it to bring resuscitating or healing.

The law, then, is compliance with the universal spiritual influence that awakens any atomic center to the necessity of its concurrent activity in relationships to other pathological forces or influences within a given body. Whether this is by spiritual forces, by any of the mechanical forces, it is of necessity one and the same. Many are the divisions or characters of those ills that befall or become a portion of each individual body. Some are set in motion so that certain portions of the glandular system or of the organs of the body perform more than their share. Hence some are thin, some are fat, some are tall, some are short.

What said He? Can anyone by taking thought make one hair white or black, or add one cubit to his stature? WHO giveth healing, then?     It is in any manner the result only of compliance to the First Cause, and the activity of same within the individual's *relative* relation to its own evolution.

Ready for questions.

**Q-1.** *Is group action more effective than individual, and if so, why?*

**A-1.** "Where two or three are gathered in my name, I am in the midst of them." These words were spoken by Life, Light, Immortality, and are based on a law. For, in union is strength. Why?

Because as there is oneness of purpose, oneness of desire, it becomes motivative within the active forces or influences of a body. The multiplicity of ideas may make confusion, but added cords of strength in one become of the nature as to increase the *ability* and influence in every expression of such a law.

**Q-2.** *In any form of psychic healing, is an etheric intermediary employed?*

**A-2.** Possible; but the etheric body of the individual seeking or finding expression must be in accord with that which draws upon such an influence.

**Q-3.** *In certain types of insanity, is there an etheric body involved? If so, how?*

**A-3.** Possession.

Let's for the moment use examples that may show what has oft been expressed from here:

There is the physical body, there is the mental body, there is the soul body. They are One, as the Trinity; yet these may find a manner of expression that is individual unto themselves. The body itself finds its own level in its *own* development. The mind, through anger, may make the body do that which is contrary to the better influences of same; it may make for a change in its environ, its surrounding, contrary to the laws of environment or hereditary forces that are a portion of the *élan vital* of each manifested body, with the spirit or the soul of the individual.

Then, through pressure upon some portion of the anatomical structure that would make for the disengaging of the natural flow of the mental body through the physical in its relationships to the soul influence, one may be dispossessed of the mind; thus ye say rightly he is "out of his mind."

Or, where there are certain types of characters of disease found in various portions of the body, there is the lack of the necessary *vital* for the resuscitating of the energies that carry on through brain structural forces of a given body. Thus disintegration is produced, and ye call it dementia praecox—by the very smoothing of the indentations necessary for the rotary influences or vital force of the spirit within same to find expression. Thus derangements come.

Such, then, become possessed as of hearing voices, because of their closeness to the borderland. Many of these are termed deranged when they may have more of a closeness to the universal than one who may be standing nearby and commenting; yet they are awry when it comes to being normally balanced or healthy for their activity in a material world.

**Q-4.** *Is it possible to give any advice as to how an individual may raise his own vibrations, or whatever may be necessary, to effect a self-cure?*

**A-4.** By raising that attunement of self to the spirit within, that is of the soul body—about which we have been speaking.

Oft in those conditions where necessary ye have seen produced within a body unusual or abnormal strength, either for physical or mental activity. From whence arose such? *Who* hath given thee power? Within what live ye? *What* is Life? It is the *attuning* of self, then, to same. *How?*

As the body-physical is purified, as the mental body is made wholly at-one with purification or purity, with the life and light within itself, healing comes, strength comes, power comes.

So may an individual effect a healing, through meditation, through attuning not just a side of the mind nor a portion of the body but the whole, to that at-oneness with the spiritual forces within, the gift of the life-force within each body.

For (aside, please), when matter comes into being, what has taken place? The Spirit ye worship as God has *moved* in space and time to make for that which gives its expression; perhaps as wheat, as corn, as flesh, as whatever may be the movement in that ye call time and space.

Then *making* self in an at-onement with that Creative Force brings what? That necessary for the activity which has been set in motion and has become manifested to be in accord *with* that First Cause.

Hence do we find it becomes necessary that ye speak, ye act, that way. For whosoever cometh to offer to self, or to make an offering to the Throne of mercy or grace, and speaketh unkind of his brother, is one partially awake or aware.

For that which has brought distraughtness, distress, disease in the earth, or in manifestation, is transgression of the law.

We are through for the present. 281-24

# FULFILLING YOUR IDEALS IN LIFE

*by Mark A. Thurston, Ph.D.*

We all have set high ideals for ourselves on this journey we call our spiritual path. Inspired by the lives of great teachers and servants of God, we set for ourselves aspirations to fulfill the potential of our spiritual heritage. We formulate specific objectives in terms of physical attunement and loving acts. We identify ideal mental states—harmonious and integrative attitudes and emotions. Each of us selects a central motivating spirit which we hope will fully direct our lives—a spiritual ideal.

As important as the process is which leads to clearly defined ideals, the work has only begun at that point. The journey is long and full of temptations and challenges. In order to fulfill ideals successfully, we need persistence, courage, and wisdom. Frequently, we will have the opportunity to settle for something less or to forget what we have set for ourselves. Too early we can misinterpret the opportunities with which life presents us.

The Cayce readings were often helpful to individuals by giving advice and counsel about how to go about most effectively living the ideals which have been set. A good illustration of this process is found in the sixth reading obtained for (622) in February of 1941. This man was a 35-year-old clerk/bookkeeper. His previous readings included a life reading in which specific past-life experiences and influences were described. In reading 622-6 he sought "counsel, advice and guidance as to how he may best fulfill the purpose for entering this experience."

Both from the background information and from specific

statements in the reading, it seems evident that (622) is a very talented individual, especially in the areas of music and voice. The advice in the reading then becomes focused on how he can clarify his purposes and ideals, and outlines a many-faceted formula for how to go about fulfilling those ideals. Each of us can easily imagine that this reading was given to us personally since the concepts and principles set forth have an especially fine quality of depth and general applicability.

In the first portion of the reading, stress is placed upon clarity of purpose and ideal. The reading insists that "definite choices be made"—that is a statement which addresses a tendency in most all of us to straddle the fence and maintain a variety of motivating influences in life. This provides the convenience of situational consciousness: In one set of circumstances we can react with one type of central, life movitation; in another set of circumstances, with a different motivation. What this creates is "the warring of one phase of the consciousness with another," a state which the reading apparently perceived was going on within (622) himself.

A key reason why a unity of purpose and ideal is required relates to the interconnections of body, mind, and spirit. Because they are knit so closely together, they react as if one. For example, we mislead ourselves if we think that we can have a motivation of resentment in our mental bodies and not feel its impact on our physical bodies. We are inviting disharmony if we think we can hold the motivation of gratification in relation to our physical bodies and not have it affect our attitudinal or emotional state (i.e., the mental body) or the spiritual body.

The reading advises both (622) and us that what is needed is a harmony of ideals in which the motivations directing our physical and mental bodies are congruent with the deepest sense of purposefulness of the spirit. One of the ways in which we easily fail in this effort stems from a misinterpretation of our material surroundings. As an example, the reading cites the teaching of Jesus: "who, by taking thought, can turn one hair black or white, or change one whit in the material experience?" And then it goes on to say that this teaching is often misinterpreted. Perhaps it is frequently misunderstood by men and women to mean "just enjoy the physical plane and take from it all you can get." This option may be tempting, especially when we work hard with a high ideal and the material surroundings of our lives do not appear to respond.

**. . . there are periods when in making choices of activities that the material surroundings do not always coordinate (apparently) with the entity's ideal. Yet, as was given again, in whatsoever state an entity, an individual finds himself, *that* is necessary for his individual development! This is another way of saying, "Seek and ye shall find; knock and it will be opened unto you."**

**For, all that is necessary in an individual entity's fulfilling the purpose for which it entered an experience is present in the entity's particular environ . . .**

This excerpt contains the first key principle concerning the fulfillment of our ideals. We must look upon our material lives from a proper perspective. Keeping in mind the often stated formula from the readings—"the spiritual is the life, the mental is the builder, the material is the result"—we should appreciate the delay that may occur between the building and the results. Material appearance always lags behind consciousness, sometimes only seconds and at other times months or years. There is little hope in our ever fulfilling ideals if we become impatient and frustrated with the lack of apparent coordination between growth in consciousness and the manifestation of results. One spiritual teacher of Tibetan Buddhism, Lama Anagarika Govinda, has even pointed out that the material life often seems alien to those who are progressing rapidly in consciousness growth. This is *not* so much a matter of the seeker having rejected the physical plane but rather a byproduct of how the laws of cause, effect and manifestation work.

At the same time, this reading points out that what we *are* experiencing from material conditions still has great meaning for us. Just as a nocturnal dream may be the product of past experiences and yet have great meaning for you in the present, today's physical life conditions may be the manifestation of your consciousness of the past, yet still have important meaning and growth opportunity for your consciousness of the present.

Each of our growth opportunities is some aspect of the

# Discover the wealth of information in the Edgar Cayce readings

Dreams
Soul Mates
Karma
Earth Changes
Universal Laws
Meditation
Holistic Health
ESP
Astrology
Atlantis
Psychic Development
Numerology
Pyramids
Death and Dying
Auto-Suggestion
Reincarnation
Akashic Records
Planetary Sojourns
Mysticism
Spiritual Healing
And other topics

## Membership Benefits You Receive Each Month

---

EDGAR CAYCE FOUNDATION and
A.R.E. LIBRARY/VISITORS CENTER
Virginia Beach, Va.
*OVER 50 YEARS OF SERVICE*

call to be a co-creator with God. But how are we to decide the best way to respond to those opportunities? Our vision is often clouded when we face such choices. We do not see clearly which options lead to greater co-creativity with the Divine and which lead to greater separation from God. But at this point, the reading offers (622) (and us as well) a standard by which to evaluate our choices.

> Thus, if the choice leads the entity into the exalting of self, it becomes as naught in the end. If the choice is that self is to be used in whatever manner—as in the talents, the attributes, the associations with its fellow men—to *glorify* the Creative Force, then the body, the mind, finds that peace, that harmony, that *purpose* for which it chose to enter a material experience.

Perhaps more than anything else it is self-exaltation which will stand in the way and keep us from the fulfillment of our ideals. The counterpart—a willingness to be used to glorify God, caring not who gets the credit—is sure to be a key ingredient for us all in fulfilling our soul's purpose.

It is always the mind which stands as the mediator between the world of spirit (and our high ideals) on the one hand and the world of material expression on the other. In the counsel given to (622), the reading warns, "For, as the tree is bent, so does it grow." The metaphor is equivalent to a Biblical version which the readings often quoted as well: "As a tree falls, there will it lie." Both images are designed to instruct us about how the set or orientation of the mind determines the subsequent experience.

This principle is graphically demonstrated in many reported experiences as people make alterations in consciousness—what is held in mind during the transition largely determines the content of the subsequent experience. For example, an attitude held in mind as one falls asleep will very likely play a considerable role in shaping the dreams of that night. Or, one's attitudes and beliefs about death and the nature of the after-death state may greatly influence the quality of experience on the other side.

The same principle operates in daily experiences, even when we are not making dramatic alterations in levels of consciousness. As the mental body is biased or predisposed in a particular direction ("as the tree is bent"), our material lives proceed to unfold in that same direction ("so does it grow"). According to this reading, the point at which we must try to catch the process is right at the bend, awakening to those usually unconscious moments of "urges . . . seeking to gratify this or that phase . . ." Unfortunately, we usually wait until the branch or limb has grown out, and forever dissatisfied with the way our lives are going, we continually try to saw limbs off our tree.

These bends in the tree can be likened to the karmic patterns within us—automatic urges and impulses that can lead our lives toward particular phases of unfoldment which may not match our ideals. How are we to resist the influence of these patterns, of these bends? No doubt this was a question with which (622) had wrestled in efforts to live his ideals. The advice given to him in the reading is dramatic and introduces a very significant principle in the Cayce readings' philosophy of the salvation of souls: "Thus does He . . . *become* thy way, and become that termed by some thy karma."

We can, as it were, trade in *our* karma for the karma of the Christ. We can use free will to surrender our predispositions of attitude and emotion—our fears, guilts, resentments, and insecurities. In exchange, we may elect to take on the predisposition built by the Christ—His patterns and His karma. It doesn't mean that we must literally be crucified in the physical body if we make this choice; but it does mean we will have to surrender and sacrifice.

This is the straight and narrow way to the fulfillment of our ideals. It may be that all other ways are merely winding roads which parallel this way. Or perhaps it is that all other ways eventually lead back to this one. The principle—or the invitation to experience the principle, which is in the reading's counsel—suggests that of himself this man is not likely to fulfill his ideals and soul's purpose. He needs the powerful influence of something beyond himself. Then there can come real hope that this lifetime will be one of great fulfillment.

The remaining portion of the reading's initial discourse (i.e., before the question-and-answer section) is an extraordinary description of specific consciousness tools which can be used to help fulfill ideals. Again the quality of the suggestions to (622) indicates that these are universal techniques which can work for anyone. Seven specific approaches are included.

1. *Consciously insert a new pattern to replace a karmic one.* This technique is introduced by defining karma as "giving way to impulse." In other words, when we think, feel, or act impulsively, we are living our lives almost unconsciously and there can be little hope for realizing our ideals. However, if one consciously chooses a different sort of response pattern—such as holding in mind or saying an affirmation that corresponds to one's ideal—then life can unfold quite differently. The reading even cites an example of the way (622) already was doing this occasionally. It refers to his aptitudes with music and voice, saying "when the entity has sung Halleluiah it was much harder to say 'dammit.' "

2. *Invite the Christ to be your companion in all that you do.* It is noted that "even under stress" this principle holds true. Perhaps it was true of (622), and is a tendency of our own, to forget the nearness of God when daily life pressures push in on us. The key is *our* invitation, our willingness to ask.

> **Invite Him, by name, by purpose, by desire, to be thy companion in all that ye do, all that ye say. He rejecteth not those who willingly, honestly, sincerely, invite Him to be with them. As He never rejected an invitation by any as He walked in the earth as an individual, neither does He reject the invitation of a soul that *seeks*—in sincerity—His companionship.**

3. *Draw upon the inner knowledge you already have of the reality of God and your ideal.* Our tendency is to conceptualize our ideals and our God as something far from our experience. Yet here the counsel of the reading is to remember that we already know God—within us is the memory of direct experience with Him. "For thou knowest the way—thou hast heard, thou hast seen, yea thou hast tasted of the Lord and hast *found* Him good!"

One way of interpreting this advice is that in past lives (622) had already experienced directly the reality of God and in this lifetime he is encouraged to reawaken that memory. But such direct experience need not be limited merely to physical incarnations. Many of us no doubt have had parallel experiences in other dimensions of consciousness and such memories can potentially be reawakened to aid our current work of fulfilling ideals.

4. *Glorify the good in all that you encounter.* This fundamental rule of the spiritual life is naturally part of the formula for fulfilling ideals. The first phase of this approach is to minimize "the faults in all, glorifying the good thou seest in everyone." Apparently there is something inherent in the tendency to bring faults to the foreground of our perceptions which, in turn, stifles our own growth. Perhaps when our outlook magnifies the imperfections of others, it sets up within ourselves a corresponding process of activating patterns within us which block our own talents and ideals from manifesting.

For example, suppose a man invests considerable energy in another person's shortcoming. Having invested energy in that fasion, he has now magnetized his own conscious mind in such a way that it will pull from the depths of his own unconscious life the patterns and habits which resemble the very shortcoming in his neighbor. If the neighbor's shortcoming is narrow-mindedness, then the fault-finding man is likely to encounter his own patterns of bias and rigidity coming into play more often. We are counseled not to find fault in others both because it makes things harder for that person to grow *and* change and because it is counterproductive for ourselves.

However, this principle goes on deeper in its challenge, as the reading instructs, "And when ye succeed in seeing the good or the beautiful in a living man, a living object that ye even hate, *then* ye may know ye are taking hold on the Lord!" In other words, if we want to be successful in our desire to fulfill ideals, we must go beyond merely avoiding fault-finding. To recognize the core of light and good in someone you have come to hate serves to magnetize the conscious mind to a higher consciousness. But in this instance the conscious life draws into awareness the action of grace—talents and abilities and influences of healing are drawn from the depths of the soul.

5. *Let go of the things which trouble and beset you.* This approach in consciousness is particularly recommended in the reading for those things in life for which we condemn ourselves. So often these are things from the past—misfortunes of commission or omission—for which we have not forgiven ourselves. We need a sense of freedom from

such doubts and guilts if we are to be able to move on in growth toward an ideal.

It may be difficult to let go of our troubled state of mind. Self-condemnation may have become familiar, even a part of our daily routine. Despite its familiarity, we must learn to release and let go, "leaving behind those things that would so easily beset."

6. *Stay focused on the positive.* As potent as doubts and fears can be in their resistance to our ideals, nothing is accomplished by fighting them at their own level. The reading encourages us to keep focused upon the best that we know—to "turn thy face to the light"—if we wish to move toward our ideals. "The shadows of doubt and fear" may still remain but not in a position which can block our progress.

7. *Act as a channel for something bigger than self.* This final approach for fulfilling our ideals is found in the question-and-answer portion of the reading. The question posed by (622) concerns his sense of unfulfillment regarding his musical performances. Clearly he has an ideal in mind, to be able to express to others "exactly what (his) heart wishes to do." The solution proposed in the reading is that he develop more of a sense of being a channel. "Hence when ye sing, when ye speak, when ye approach thy friend or foe in such a way and manner that He speaketh *through* thee, have ye 'gone over big'? It will never die!"

Following this seven-step formula, the reading addresses several questions, three of which contain particularly useful advice to us all. The first addresses the question of *how* to approach a difficult decision in life. For (622) it was a matter of whether or not to find a way out of armed services induction: "In what way have I fallen short . . . to prevent induction in (the) army service?" The Cayce reading's answer is probably appropriate to whatever personal dilemma any of us might face.

> This becomes, now, a choice in self . . . Put this rather in this light, this manner:
> . . . is it not the better way to talk it over with Him? And say, "Lord, here am I! Can, or may, or will I be of greater service to *Thee*, to my fellow man, to my country in following the option I contemplate? (For (622), this was military service.) Or may I be of the greater service in other channels?" And leave it with Him!

**If ye are sincere, if ye are in earnest, if ye will use thy talents, let *Him* direct thy way!**

It is, then, a willingness to be shown what is best that is the key. We can be guided if we keep an attunement with the ideal (i.e., to be of service, as in this man's case) and ask to be directed to the method and form that will best allow that ideal to be fulfilled.

The second especially significant question involves advice about using what one has at hand, this one concerning changing to another department at his job. The reading counsels to "Be what thou shouldest be *where* thou art! And when thou hast proven *thyself,* He will give thee the better ways!" It is a frequent human tendency to look for greener pastures when we desire to fulfill a dream and ideal. But the philosophy in this and many other Cayce readings is that the opportunities presented by the current conditions and circumstances of life are especially designed and afford the opportunity to move forward with our ideals. Not that the current conditions and circumstances will exist forever; when we have fulfilled the best we can do with what is at hand, the next step will be presented. This principle is presented again when (622) asked whether or not to establish a vocal school. The answer in the reading was: "These will come of themselves."

This should not be understood as a call to passivity but rather to patience and wisdom. We are invited to be assertive and active but primarily within the realm of our own inner responses to those opportunities life presents. We are encouraged to be active and to use free will to make changes. But the most necessary change is usually the one which alters our own attitudes or behaviors—moving us toward the best we can possibly do with the current challenges.

Finally, in one other highlight from the question-and-answer portion, the reading makes the distinction between the personality and the individuality in one's life. Drawing upon definitions used in many other Cayce readings, we can think of the personality as the outer appearance of what we seem to be (i.e., what we would have others think we are), whereas the individuality is that deeper, more real core of being which says "I am." If the ideals that we have set are attuned to the spirit, then those ideals have their inception in the individuality of oneself. Certainly, the personality needs to be involved in their fulfillment, but it is from this deeper center that our motivations in life can arise as we seek to manifest high ideals. That center is described as a place within us that is "more gracious (i.e., full of grace), more humble, in *all* thy dealings with thy fellow man." This basic distinction between personality and individuality is a fitting summary and conclusion. Living from one's individuality is the basic strategy recommended by the readings for the fulfillment of ideals.

# Reading Number 622-6 _____

*This psychic reading given by Edgar Cayce at his home on Arctic Crescent, Virginia Beach, Va., this 6th day of February, 1941 . . .*

*Hugh Lynn Cayce: You will have before you the body and enquiring mind of (622), present in this room, who seeks a mental and spiritual reading, with counsel, advice and guidance as to how he may best fulfill the purpose for entering this experience. You will answer the questions he submits, as I ask them.*

Mr. Cayce: Yes, we have the body, the enquiring mind, (622), present in this room.

In giving advice or counsel, in fulfilling one's purpose for entering a material experience, much of that as has been the basis for the entrance—or the choice of the entity in entering—must be taken into consideration; as well as the premises from which such reasoning might be stated.

For, the answer to all such, necessarily, must arise from the individual self and its purposes, its desires, its hopes, its fears, its failures, its faults.

The entity finds self in the present with a body, a mind, and the hopes and experiences of a soul. Each phase of the entity's experience in the present, then, has its attributes, its weaknesses and its strength.

As the body then is the temple of the living God (to the

entity), thus it becomes necessary that definite choices be made by the entity as to what are the ideals—of body, of mind, of soul. For, these in the physical reactions are one, if their purposes are one; yet confusions constantly arise in the experience of the entity owing to the warring of one phase of the consciousness with another; causing oft the exercising of choice as to courses to pursue, or manners of approach to conditions or circumstances that arise in the experience of the entity.

Thus, as the entity may find, as it takes cognizance of such experiences, the full intent or purpose was indicated by the Teacher of teachers—that who, by taking thought, can turn one hair black or white, or change one whit in the material experience? This is oft misinterpreted. As the individual entity finds in the experience, there are periods when in making choices of activities that the material surroundings do not always coordinate (apparently) with the entity's ideal. Yet, as was given again, in whatsoever state an entity, an individual finds himself, *that* is necessary for his individual development! This is another way of saying, "Seek and ye shall find; knock and it will be opened unto you."

For, all that is necessary in an individual entity's fulfilling the purpose for which it entered an experience is present in the entity's particular environ, in its particular outlook upon this complex condition that is experienced by each soul.

As is understood, that which is mental arises from those abilities innate and manifested in life's expression itself—as in the fact that *every* phase of life is the image of the Creator, or has the ability within itself to *create* itself; thus the ability to make its own environment, if the activity for such is in keeping with the pattern *of* the ideal the entity has chosen.

Thus it becomes each soul—in its realization, in its awareness, in its seeking—to know the Author of its ideal—spiritually, mentally, materially. The spiritual is the life, the mental is the builder, the material is the result of that builded through the purposes held by the individual entity.

Then, the entity finds himself as a co-creator with the Divine that is manifested in self. Thus, if the choice leads the entity into the exalting of self, it becomes as naught in the end. If the choice is that self is to be used in whatever manner—as in the talents, the attributes, the associations with its fellow men—to *glorify* the Creative Force, then the body, the mind, finds that peace, that harmony, that *purpose* for which it chose to enter a material experience.

Then, to the entity, it might be easily said, "Go *thou* and put that principle into thy daily practice."

Yet, from the experiences of this entity through the material sojourns in the earth, there comes those things, those urges for a seeking to gratify this or that phase of its material manifestations. For, as the tree is bent, so does it grow.

Yet *know* that thy body is the temple of the *living* God; *there* ye may seek communion! There ye may seek counsel as to the choices to be made, the directions to be taken!

Thus does He—as in His promise, "Lo, I am with thee always, unto the end"—*become* thy way, and become that termed by some thy karma.

What is karma but giving way to impulse? Just as has been experienced by this entity, when the entity has sung Halleluiah it was much harder to say "dammit."

Hence we find that, even under stress, He goeth *with* thee—*all* the way. For as He has given, "If ye will but ask, I will come—I will *abide*—I will be with thee!"

Thus may the entity use its abilities, its talents, its voice. For, know that all thy attributes and activities of the senses are the gifts of God. This is true with every entity, but especially with this entity. For he that sings, he that sees, he that speaks, he that hears well is especially *gifted* of God; and not only has the one or the two but the five talents that may be made into such measures—by the choice of the entity—that he may be ruler not only over the five senses but the ten kingdoms in God's own way!

Then it may be said, study thou—in thy mental, in thy spiritual self—to show thyself approved unto Him. For thou knowest the way—thou hast heard, thou hast seen, yea thou hast tasted of the Lord and hast *found* Him good!

Study then to show thyself approved unto thy Ideal, that is in Christ Jesus, the Lord; dividing the words of truth in their proper relationships; finding not fault—as this means—but rather minimizing the faults in all, glorifying the good thou seest in everyone.

And when ye succeed in seeing the good or the beautiful in a living man, a living object that ye even hate, *then* ye may know that ye are taking hold on the Lord!

Keep self unspotted from the world; condemning not thyself, then, but rather leaving behind those things that would so easily beset. Turn thy face to the light in Him always and the shadows of doubt and fear will fall far behind.

Press *on* to the mark of the higher calling as set in *Him, and* in *thee*—if ye walk, if ye talk often with Him. Invite Him, by name, by purpose, by desire, to be thy companion in all that ye do, all that ye say. He rejecteth not those who willingly, honestly, sincerely, invite HIm to be with them. As He never rejected an invitation by any as He walked in the earth as an individual, neither does He reject the invitation of a soul that *seeks*—in sincerity—His companionship.

Ready for questions.

**Q-1.** *Am I using my opportunities as stepping-stones or stumbling stones?*

**A-1.** *Who* is to judge but thou? What measuring stick usest thou in thy search for truth?

**Q-2.** *In what way have I fallen short in correlating my muscular injuries and the influences of my present labors to prevent induction in army service?*

**A-2.** This becomes, now, a choice in self. Here ye are faced with a problem. Put this rather in this light, this manner:

As ye seek ye *may* so command, so demand of thy associates, as to be refused for service. But rather in the light of that just indicated, is it not the better way to talk it over with Him? And say, "Lord, here am I! Can, or may, or will I be of greater service to *Thee*, to my fellow man, to my country, in following the option I contemplate? Or may I be of the greater service in other channels? And leave it with Him!

If ye are sincere, if ye are in earnest, if ye will use thy talents, let *Him* direct thy way!

**Q-3.** *Will I or will I not be accepted for army duty? If so, where should I try to be located?*

**A-3.** Let this be answered in the first, see?

**Q-4.** *Outline specific activities for next few years whereby I may carry out my ideal.*

**A-4.** We've been trying to tell you so for the last thirty-two minutes!

**Q-5.** *Will the activities along present line of endeavor [at government base] be more beneficial in future years, or should I seek a change in other departments? Explain.*

**A-5.** Be what thou shouldest be *where* thou art! And when thou hast proven *thyself,* He will give thee the better ways!

Has it not been indicated that thou hast not only the one or the two but the five talents? Thus He expects much of thee!

**Q-6.** *Should I continue my studies with Werrenrath?*
**A-6.** Yes.

**Q-7.** *Is there any other branch of endeavor that should be taken up in conjunction with my music which would give a wider scope for my expression to masses?*
**A-7.** The ways and manners and means of personality versus individuality; or in being more gracious, more humble, in *all* thy dealings with thy fellow man.

**Q-8.** *When, if ever, should I definitely start a career with my voice, as in singing, and give up my regular employment?*
**A-8.** You've already begun! Just keep on keeping on!

**Q-9.** *How much longer will it be before radio will be a definite channel through which I may be able to reach the masses?*
**A-9.** Before the year is out, if you go on with the induction and apply self in that direction!

**Q-10.** *Why do I always have the feeling that I cannot "put over" to an audience just exactly what my heart wishes to do?*
**A-10.** Doubt! Talk oftener with Him. Though ye may oft feel, as from man's viewpoint, that ye can never put it over *wholly*—yet it has been, it will indeed be as He gave, "The world may pass away, but my word shall *not* pass away."

Hence when ye sing, when ye speak, when ye approach thy friend or foe in such a way and manner that He speaketh *through* thee, have ye "gone over big"? It will never die!

**Q-11.** *Should I establish a vocal school, or seek other singing jobs?*
**A-11.** These will come of themselves. Eventually the school would be well, but this would be in forty-five or forty-six ('45 or '46).

**Q-12.** *When should I start to establish a residence of my own?*
**A-12.** When ye think ye are capable of doing so!

**Q-13.** *Married or single state?*
**A-13.** A home alone isn't very much a home!

**Q-14.** *When should I begin turning the 5th post for my bed?*

**A-14.** When ye have prepared yourself in the better manner.

**Q-15.** *Whom should I contact in order to get the best results for the sale of the timber on the land owned jointly by my family in Elizabeth City?*

**A-15.** Greenpoint Lumber.

**Q-16.** *Will it ever be possible for me to retrieve any of my inheritance known as the Jennings estate? If so, how? (Where will I find correlated records of definite proof of my ancestors, on my father's side, to establish my claim to the Jennings fortune?)*

**A-16.** Not after *this* war is through!

**Q-17.** *Please analyze a method as to how to go about to analyze myself.*

**A-17.** Take the yardstick of the Master's. As He gave, "A new commandment give I unto you, that ye love one another."

We are through for the present.

622-6

# USING TALENTS OF THE SOUL

by Mark A. Thurston, Ph.D.

One of the great services provided by the Edgar Cayce readings was to help individuals recognize talents and abilities. In hundreds of mental/spiritual or "life readings" the source of the information was able to describe insightfully both the talents within the soul *and* what one needed to do for those talents to flower.

The skill and wisdom of the Cayce readings to do this are beautifully illustrated in the example of reading 3420-1. This 57-year-old woman is described (in the background of the case) as a divorced writer who wrote to Edgar Cayce in April, 1943, after she read *There Is a River.* She requested a reading and asked that it address certain problems. "Here is my difficulty. I can't write *enough.* I get ideas and then some blocks keep me from writing . . . I am not happy— which undoubtedly is my own fault. Partly fear because I don't write enough—or make enough money. Partly because I am alone."

From a universal perspective what did the source of the Cayce readings see for this woman? Clearly she seemed disappointed and frustrated with her life; she seemed to have a certain aptitude for writing, but it wasn't working out for her.

The reading begins with a remarkable general discourse about soul purpose and soul growth. It is noteworthy for its clarity and depth—clearly material which was meant to be helpful to (3420), but is generally applicable as well. The initial picture that is painted in the reading is of the soul as custodian of humanity's possibilities and probabilities. In other words, the soul has within itself many possible directions—some leading toward growth and others toward retardment in consciousness.

But how are we to judge whether or not decisions are being made which lead to soul *growth*? The reading cautions that (3420) (and we as well) cannot easily determine such by the outward criterion of material success.

> **Then, as to whether there is the development or retarding of the soul-entity, is dependent upon the manner in which the abilities of the entity are exercised or used.**
>
> **Not all that is considered by some as material success is soul success. Not all that is soul development, as considered in other spheres, is considered material success.**
>
> **For each soul enters the material experience with opportunities in the abilities that have been attained or acquired as a part of the individuality and personality of the entity. Each soul-entity enters with that hope of preparing itself for closer or greater communion with its first cause or first purpose.**

In the third paragraph of the passage quoted above, additional principles are introduced. First, the emphasis is upon the universality of soul talents—"each soul enters" the physical plane with talents, skills, and abilities which it has opportunities to express. In other words, even though this particular reading will focus on the ways that (3420) herself can use talents such as writing for soul growth, we *all* have talents which will give us similar opportunities.

The final sentence of the quoted excerpt presents another key principle—that each soul is born into material life with an impetus for drawing closer to God. Yes, we may be magnetized or drawn back into physical form because of karmic desires, but that is not the whole story. Deep within us—no matter how karmic the patterns that have pulled us back to physical incarnation—there is also a profound impetus to experience growth in consciousness. That impetus may be buried or forgotten but it remains there. And the opportunities with which our soul talents provide us may be a way to reawaken it.

The reading then continues with a further description of the universal challenges facing this woman. The central focus is described in terms of choice. "There is ever set before this entity daily (as each entity), good and evil, life and death."

But how are we to understand these polarities which have puzzled theologians and philosophers for centuries? In simple terms, the reading equates "life" with growth. The student of this particular discourse might well wish that an elaboration of this statement would have been made. And it was, but later in the reading when the source once again raises the issue of growth: "And unless each soul entity . . . makes the world better . . . the life is a failure; especially so far as growth is concerned." Our sense of life, then, must be inextricably linked with that of others. If life is growth and if there is no real experience of growth unless one has lived to make things better for others, then the choice of "life" is the choice to use our talents in service to others.

But what of the other option? Each day we have the chance to choose death, which the reading equates with "separation or . . . turning away from." That kind of choice to be apart from can refer to the relationship we have with our own soul talents, with other people, or with God.

The reading goes on to stress the importance of *will*. But here a novel feature of the will is proposed. Rather than portray the will as merely that which allows us to make choices, the reading incorporates the qualities of knowledge and understanding as well. "Hence the entity has in itself *will*, that knowledge, that understanding, with which the entity exercises its choice . . ." This is quite a different notion of will than we may be used to working with. Most frequently will is described in terms of "willpower" which emphasizes the negative side of things (e.g., to use one's will-(power) to refrain from an extra dessert or to keep from criticizing someone). But here we find phrases which suggest a different point of view—will is linked to that within us that knows and understands what is needed. Choices then flow as a natural result of what we consciously see is best, rather than from holding back from what we have decided is wrong.

This principle takes on greater importance when we consider that our tendency is usually to analyze and work on self in terms of perceived faults: weaknesses and vices. We end up trying to use what we call "will" to refrain from these tendencies. But if the will is viewed in a more positive way, it means that which allows us "that knowledge, that understanding" of the good within, of the soul talents within. Then the choices that flow naturally can be those which give expression to our talents.

This perspective of the will is found in other writings, sometimes explained more fully or within a metaphor which helps us keep it in mind. P.D. Ouspensky (a writer frequently recommended in the Cayce readings) described the feel of exercising real will as the same sense that one has upon suddenly seeing the solution to a difficult mathematical problem. In other words, it is a quality of knowledge and understanding which allows us to make effective choices.

The reading seems most concerned about (3420)'s choices regarding the free and clear use of soul talents which have heretofore been encumbered by limiting habits. The reading continually encourages her to recognize the creative talents of her soul but cautions her about how they may become adulterated or misused.

For example, this woman is told that in addition to being a very vivacious, outgoing person, she is also blessed with the talent of being a sensitive listener to others. The reading continues:

> **But in the periods of listening it is paralleling, measuring or analyzing those about the entity. But what is thy standard with which ye analyze thy neighbor, thy brother? Ask self these questions. Do ye use the same standard that ye would desire to be measured by? For as the law is, with what measure ye mete, it is measured to thee again. If the entity uses such a yardstick in its judgments of others, greater will be the ability of the entity to influence others by what it says or does.**

The reading has identified a soul pattern—both a talent (sensitive listener) and a habit that keeps that talent from being used for growth. The habit is to measure and analyze by inconsistent standards; and the recommendation from the reading is a gentle reminder, a gentle turning of her consciousness, so that the talent can truly be used to influence others for good.

Continuing its analysis of her soul patterns, the reading describes her as one who possesses talents related to art and music—elements which are a part of "the entity's innate and manifested individuality." The term "individuality" is significant here because of the distinct way in which the Cayce readings as a whole use this word. In contrast to the "personality" (which is called "that (which) one desires others to see in self" (294-185)), the "individuality" has a quality of permanence and deeper reality ("the soul's relationship to . . . its ideal" (294-185)). In other words, the reading is attempting to identify patterns which are a profound part of (3420)'s being, and not just superficial likes and dislikes which her personality may have taken on from her present surroundings and associations. It is these innate talents of the soul's *individuality* with which we are to concern ourselves.

Here we have the blending of two distinct soul talents. One is the capacity to express herself in words as a writer—a talent to be an effective analyzer and then to give written form to it. The other talent is a sensitivity to harmony, beauty, music and art. This blending of soul talents is explained in the reading as it describes *what kind* of writer to be.

**Hence the entity in its abilities as a writer may use such, rather than its description of things as things. For instance, in describing a rose, its color, its harmony, its beauty may be described rather than so tall, so short, so wide or so big . . .**

**The entity may describe, then, the vibration of a city, rather than its streets or its lights or its parks. For these are the activities that impress themselves upon this entity.**

The question of how to use innate abilities is *far broader than just vocational choice.* The way in which soul talents can be blended illustrates this. In its counsel, this Cayce reading goes beyond saying merely that there are talents of analysis and verbal expression, and, therefore, be a writer. There is a subtlety in the reading which couples and blends strengths of the soul to recommend distinct qualities and nuances that may be brought to her life's work. Without those nuances she may never feel fulfilled in life. In this instance, the woman was already a writer, but a frustrated one; and the reading is calling her to a new sense of purpose and focus—inviting her to incorporate other soul talents. She would make an excellent art, music or literature critic, especially if she is careful to use a loving standard by which to make her evaluations.

At this point, the source of the reading shifts its orientation and begins to describe astrological influences upon her pyschological makeup. Those familiar with the Cayce life readings will recall that astrological influences are linked to interplanetary sojourns—the experience the soul has in other dimensions of consciousness between physical incarnations in the three-dimensional plane. The developments and inclinations from these interplanetary sojourns especially relate to mental aptitudes, whereas our emotional sensitivities and tendencies are the result of previous experiences in the physical plane. This is not to imply that neither development nor change in mental attributes can take place while physically incarnated; but rather that the primary tendency of attitude and mental orientation most often arises from "between lifetime" experiences in nonphysical planes.

The Cayce readings suggest that each dimension of consciousness is especially designed for a specific kind of development and that the planets symbolize the various dimensions. The reading names "Mercury, Jupiter and Venus as the greater active force," identifying those aspects of consciousness (symbolized by those planets) as the origin of certain mental tendencies with which she must work. The changing configuration of these actual planets in the sky might also exert periodic influences on her— strengthening or weakening the prominence of these tendencies. For example, if a mental tendency to go to *extremes* was developed during a period of nonphysical experiencing (a dimension symbolized by Uranus), then during this earthly lifetime there might be days or weeks when the position of Uranus in the sky would tend to bring this tendency to the surface.

Because of certain astrological influences, the reading recommends two areas of discipline in life for [3420]. We might interpret these disciplines as tools for staying on track with her soul's purpose to use her talents creatively. The astrological influences—which only quicken tendencies *within herself*—might tend to move her periodically off course, leading to an unfulfilled life. The disciplines—a clarity of ideal and a budgeting of time—would keep her focused and attuned.

> **Then the more reason the entity should be very sure within self of its ideals—spiritual, mental, material. And most of all the entity should budget itself, its time. Recuperate in body, in mind, in**

**purpose, in hopes. Then, so much time should be spent in work, in labor; so much time in recreation; yea, so much time in beautifying the body.**

The reading proceeds to describe at some length a physical regimen for replenishing the physical body. Once a month for "three days in some definite week each month," she is instructed to have general hydrotherapy, massage, and any other treatments which would revitalize her body. The principle here is probably of general applicability, although the exact regimen would vary from person to person. For our soul's talents to be able to manifest, they need the physical structure which serves as a channel. A consistent commitment is needed to making the body an effective mediator of energies from the soul to the physical world and to other people.

This principle as well as the specific advice for physical revitalization appears even more important when we recall the very purpose for souls being in the earth: to bring the qualities of spirit into matter—to make finite the infinite or to spiritualize the physical. Our soul's talents are the instruments and tools we personally have available to us to do our own part in this great work. To be successful we need physical bodies as full of health and as clearly a channel as we can possibly make them.

However, the revitalization process does not stop with the physical body. The reading recommends a parallel concern for her mental body and suggests regular periods of reading, music, play, and interaction with others. This last item is especially noted because (3420) would derive great benefit from being in the midst of others' positive emotional energies.

**For it is from the emotions of others rather than from things that the entity gains and adds to the abilities of self, or is able to draw upon its abilities to be helpful for others.**

This section of the reading—the final one before specific past lives are given—concludes with a strong call to service as an ideal. It asks, "For who is the greatest?" and then answers that it is the one who is servant to all and makes each soul glad to be alive. The word "glad" is repeated in further describing this ideal: ". . . glad to have the opportunity to contribute something to the welfare of his brother."

Surely this ideal was meant for us all and not just the person who received this reading. The key to healing our planet is with a service ideal that is seen as *more than just acts of service.* As important as it is to do acts of kindness and helpfulness, an extra ingredient is needed—a sense of joyfulness and appreciation for the very opportunity to reach out to others in this way.

The reading then proceeds to describe specific past-life experiences, each of which highlights a particular soul talent or which describes a soul tendency which might influence how those talents would find expression. The most recent lifetime is depicted during the early settler days of America, when (3420) migrated to Arkansas (incidentally, the state where she was born again in 1896). But she was unhappy there and continually hoped to go back east, a desire that was fulfilled, apparently by a marriage based not on love but convenience for herself ("through (a) holy or unholy affection"). Taking up her life in the area around Baltimore, she became associated with the barnstormers.

The elements from this lifetime seem noteworthy and have a bearing on her soul's talents and how they might find expression. First is the sensitivity which the reading says she nurtured: ". . . it became a student of human nature, a student of emotions." Because of this ability it now allows her "to meet upon familiar ground those of any station in life" and would make her an especially effective writer or storyteller. The second key element is this tendency to look to the *east* to find her place of fulfillment—an inclination, we shall see, described in another past life as well.

Moving back in time, the reading then describes a lifetime in the Holy Land when, as a member of the early church in Antioch, she was one of many who were persecuted. She used certain connections that she had among Roman authorities and was able to lessen this problem of the persecution. Apparently in that lifetime as well, she was developing her soul ability as an observer and communicator: ". . . the entity became a good reporter to those varied groups and peoples there."

In another previous lifetime in the Holy Land there were patterns and tendencies built which seem to have more to do with her current aloneness than with her writing talent. She was among the tribe of Judah in Old Testament times as the building of Jersualem was being planned. "The entity was active in home building." This experience made her particularly sensitive to the love of family relations. The reading also seems to imply that it led to a sense of high idealism with her soul regarding home and family. That high idealism hadn't been met in her 20th-century lifetime and had led to strained marital relations and divorce.

**No one might describe much better than this entity the love of a mother for her babe—in words, in song, in picture. Thus home and marital relations have been strained, may be strained again.**

The final lifetime described goes back to the period just after the migration of Atlantean peoples into Egypt. Born in Egypt, but of Atlantean ancestry, the soul had certain intuitive and mystic inclinations, which might be soul talents that could still be drawn upon in connection with the central talent of observation, analysis, and writing. In that lifetime (3420) became one who worked in the Temple Beautiful and served "in the preparation of others to become emissaries; eventually going as an emissary itself to the Gobi land."

Here we see an earlier manifestation of a soul inclination to move eastward, as expressed in early America. The reading presents this as an important opportunity—that her chance to fulfill soul purpose and use her innate talents has often been linked to moving eastward from where she finds herself. The reading even suggests she consider a move to England, France, or Africa (although there is no evidence in follow-up correspondence that she ever did this). The reading concludes at this point.

In summary, there are significant principles that form an outline of what may be involved for any of us to use creatively our soul talents. (3420) had the special privilege of a reading that filled in specific details, but the essence of the outline is

1. work with talents and *blend* their strengths
2. keep a right ideal to use talents to *benefit others*
3. identify and *remove habits* that limit or distort talents, and
4. make use of karmic inclinations which may lead one to conditions or surroundings that would *stimulate* our talents to flower.

# Reading Number 3420-1 ____

*This psychic reading given by Edgar Cayce at the A.R.E. office, Arctic Crescent, Virginia Beach, Va., this 17th day of December, 1943, in accordance with request made by the self, Miss [3420] . . .*

Mr. Cayce: Yes, we have the records here of that entity now named or called [3420].

In analyzing the records as we find them here, there are many possibilities and probabilities within the realm of this entity's activity.

Then, as to whether there is the development or retarding of the soul-entity, is dependent upon the manner in which the abilities of the entity are exercised or used.

Not all that is considered by some as material success is soul success. Not all that is soul development, as considered in other spheres, is considered material success.

For each soul enters the material experience with opportunities in the abilities that have been attained or acquired as a part of the individuality and personality of the entity. Each soul-entity enters with that hope of preparing itself for closer or greater communion with its first cause or first purpose. For each soul is in the image of the Creator. And as it is in purpose spirit, it seeks to magnify or manifest the spirit of the Creator.

Hence as implied, God is spirit and seeks such to worship Him.

Thus in giving that as we find concerning this entity, these records we choose with the desire and hope and purpose that this information may be a helpful experience for the entity; enabling the entity to better fulfill those purposes for which the soul entered.

There is ever set before this entity daily (as each entity), good and evil, life and death. Life is growth. Death is as that separation or turning about, turning away from, or the opposite of growth.

Hence the entity has in itself *will*, that knowledge, that understanding, with which the entity exercises its choice, to which it adds either for the satisfying or gratifying of self's emotions or self's desires, or for the magnifying and glorifying of the spiritual sources or help.

These may be one, if the entity makes the hope, the desire of the body, the mind, the soul, in accord. Yet the soul ever seeks to magnify or glorify the Divine. Hence the constant warring that one finds in its members—body, mind, soul. These are as the (reality) of the shadows of appetites, of desires, of those things that are habits of body and that take hold as a habit. Yet who ever saw a habit? For it is a mental thing and is personal. Its individuality may be of the creative forces or of the destructive forces.

As a composite of the physical and soul urges latent and manifested with this entity, we find:

The entity is one with a pleasing personality; one very vivacious; one given to talk—at times, a great deal, and yet one who may become a good listener. But in the periods of listening it is paralleling, measuring or analyzing those about the entity. But what is thy standard with which ye analyze thy neighbor, thy brother? Ask self these questions. Do ye use the same standard that ye would desire to be measured by? For as the law is, with what measure ye mete, it is measured to thee again. If the entity uses such a yardstick in its judgments of others, greater will be the ability of the entity to influence others by what it says or does.

Also music and art are indicated as a part of the entity's innate and manifested individuality. Thus those things pertaining to the mental body, the mentality, the emotions, the purposes, the aims, the desires, those that are intangible yet are the more real for their intangibility may be drawn upon by the entity in its visualizing, in its analyzing, in its helpful influences to others. Hence the entity in its abilities as a writer may use such, rather than its description of things as things. For instance, in describing a rose, its color, its harmony, its beauty may be described rather than so tall, so short, so wide or so big.

So with any other activity of the entity in its description, use those things that are the emotions of the spirit, of the purpose, of the hope, of the desire created by the promptings, or as the prompting of an individual or a group or a mass.

The entity may describe, then, the vibration of a city, rather than its streets or its lights or its parks. For these are the activities that impress themselves upon this entity.

Thus the entity's abilities as an art critic, as a music critic, or its abilities to judge books, articles, plays, motion pictures. Every influence that appeals to the emotions and the natures of a people should be those things from and upon which the entity should draw for its helpfulness, or in that same attitude as indicated; judge as ye would be judged; magnify the virtues, minimize the faults. These ye would have thy Maker, thy God, thy ideal, thy friend, do to thee. Do ye even so to them.

As to the appearances in the earth, we find that these are a part of the great pattern through which the entity reaches this combination of emotions or characteristics.

From the astrological aspects the entity finds Mercury, Jupiter and Venus as the greater active force; while Mars might be said to be in and out.

As indicated, the entity is very vivacious, very active. Thus the entity can also rest or relax, or be as lazy as the next. Not that extreme as from Uranus, but the mystic, the artistic temperament, as it were, runs its course and must be set again if it would manifest.

Then the more reason the entity should be very sure within self of its ideals—spiritual, mental, material. And most of all the entity should budget itself, its time. Recuperate in body, in mind, in purpose, in hopes. Then, so much time should be spent in work, in labor; so much time in recreation; yea, so much time in beautifying the body. As the entity may gather, as it analyzes the cycles of that implied and indicated as to the manner in which the entity thinks and acts, at least one week out of each month should be spent in beautifying, preserving, rectifying the body—if the body would keep young, in mind, in body, in purpose. This doesn't mean that the entity should spend a whole week at nothing else, (but) choose three days out of some week in each month—not just three days in a month, but three days in some definite week each month—either the first, the second, the third or the fourth week of each month—and have the general hydrotherapy treatments, including massage, lights, and all the treatments that are in that nature of beautifying, and keeping the whole of the body-forces young.

One week each month is required for sterilizing the body functions. Then, is it a wonder that a week after such would be well for the beautifying, for the replenishing, for the supplying of the building forces for the body's activities? Supply the body mentally—so much reading should be done, so much recreation in music, so much in play and in those activities of others. For it is from the emotions of others rather than from things that the entity gains and adds to the abilities of self, or is able to draw upon its abilities to be helpful for others.

And unless each soul entity (and this entity especially) makes the world better, that corner or place of the world a little better, a little bit more hopeful, a little bit more patient, showing a little more of brotherly love, a little more of kindness, a little more of long-suffering—by the very words and deeds of the entity, the life is a failure; especially so far as growth is concerned. Though you gain the whole world, how little ye must think of thyself if ye lose the purpose for which the soul entered this particular sojourn!

Think not more highly of thyself than ye ought to think, yet no one will think more of you than you do of yourself; not in egotism, but in the desire to be of a help. For who is the greatest? He that is the servant of all, he that contributes that which makes each soul glad to be alive, glad to have the opportunity to contribute something to the welfare of his brother. These are thy virtues or thy faults, dependent upon how ye use them. The entity then naturally should ever be an optimist, not a pessimist.

The experiences in the earth have been quite varied.

Before this the entity was in the land of the present nativity during the early settlings, when the people journeyed from the western portion of Virginia and Tennessee to the land now called Arkansas.

The entity was among those who were carried along, yet never desiring, never wishing to make those changes.

Then in the name Carol McCabe, the entity forced itself to be a part of those activities, though disturbed and discouraged; until there came those periods when the entity was able—through (a) holy or unholy affection—to again come back to the eastern portion of the land.

Thus we find the entity meeting all of those hardships, yea the earthly pleasures of those early periods; become acquainted with those groups who were known in those early periods as barnstormers. The entity became a part of such in that known as Baltimore, and the name then was changed to a more glorified one—according to the entity—in those experiences.

The entity gained throughout those periods, for it became a student of human nature, a student of emotions.

Hence the abilities of the entity to meet upon familiar ground those of any station in life; the abilities as a writer, as an entertainer, the ability to tell a good story with a point or a moral, or with a question or with a lesson.

Before that the entity was in the Holy Land during those periods when there were upheavals from the persecutions of the church by those not only in high places but those who would seek to use such as a political way of attaining notoriety.

The entity was among those persecuted in Antioch. But when there was the appealing to the group to which the entity had affiliated itself, to those who had been in authority there, the entity knew Rome and the varied groups in authority. For the entity had embraced the tenets or teachings of the household of Cornelius, for it was his activities in Rome that enabled the entity to be raised to a place wherein there was less persecutions and more of that hope which the entity may apply in its experience today—in just kindness, just patience, just love.

Then the entity became a good reporter to those varied groups and peoples there. The name then was Rebba.

Before that the entity was in the Holy Land during those periods when there were divisions being made of the peoples who had entered there.

The entity was among those of the household of Judah, in those activities that sought preparations for the city that eventually became the Holy City.

The entity was active in home building. No one might describe much better than this entity the love of a mother for her babe—in words, in song, in picture. Thus home and marital relations have been strained, may be strained again. Best kept as is, then, until there is the attuning of self with those changes that may yet come into the experience of the entity. The name then was Ledeo.

Before that the entity was in the Egyptian land when there were those activities that made for the rebuilding from the turmoils that arose with the rebellions and strife.

The entity was among the Atlantean peoples, not born in Atlantis but in Egypt. Thus something of the mystic, something of the intuitive forces. And when those activities brought about the restoration, as it were, of some of the Atlantean groups, the entity entered questioningly into the services in the Temple Beautiful. These eventually became a part of the entity's activities, in the preparation of others to become emissaries; eventually going as an emissary itself to the Gobi land.

Thus those periods of change. Ever eastward, then, has been the entity's purpose—never westward. For as the changes may come in the experience of the entity, it is just the opposite from the cycle—go to the sun not with the sun. Should there be changes, then, change to England, France, Africa. For these places are yet to mean much in the rehabilitation of man for the coming events in the reorganizing of man's purpose in the earth.

As to the abilities in the life of the entity, and that to which it may attain and how:

Find self and self's relationship to Creative Forces, and apply that in relationship to thy fellow man in the measures ye would have thy Maker, thy Creator, apply mercy, judgment and love to thee . . .

3420-1

# AWAKENING THE HUMAN WILL

*by Mark A. Thurston, Ph.D.*

No faculty of the soul is more important to our spiritual quest than the will. In the model of the human soul, given to us in the Cayce readings, there are three main components: spirit, mind, and will. With each of these three there is an essential challenge to be met. In fact, most of the life readings given by Cayce contain counsel related to each one of these areas.

The essential challenge as we work with the part of the soul that is spirit is to understand oneness. Perhaps *the* fundamental principle of the Bible, the Cayce readings, and many other teachings is the oneness of all force. The spiritual energy to which we as souls have been given access has an underlying unity despite the variety of forms it may take. Frequently in readings for individuals, Cayce would identify a particular way in which the concept of oneness was to be recognized in a current, challenging situation.

The essential challenge as we work with the mind of the soul is to make it creative rather than repetitive. We are fond of quoting Cayce readings which say "Mind is the builder," and truly this is a capacity of the soul's birthright of mind. Nevertheless, our minds also have the capacity merely to repeat patterns of thought and feeling which have been built in the past. To live karmically is to be directed by old patterns of mind: memory. Life continually challenges us to respond with creativity rather than with habit. Frequently in life readings, Cayce would give specific counsel to individuals on how to do that.

But no challenge is greater than that of awakening the will.

In many ways, working with the will is a more subtle and difficult task than dealing with the mind and spirit. Because the will is so integrally linked to our very selfhood, we tend not to "see the forest for the trees" and forget that without will development there is no real enlightenment, no matter how expanded a state of mind one may reach.

The human will is that which gives us a sense of our identity as individual creations. Yes, it is that which allows us to make choices, but it is far more. To reduce will merely to "the decision maker" is to mistake the function of a quality for the quality itself. For example, while it is true that a horse can function to pull a plow, it would be a mistake to limit one's definition of a horse to this single function and fail to explore its other capabilities. In Cayce's life readings he often called the individual to an awakening of the will which was far more significant than just making effective choices in life. The challenge to use the will properly in all that it can mean is central to our search for enlightenment.

Reading 1215-4, given in 1937 for a 17-year-old boy of Christian background, well illustrates many of these points. Its structure demonstrates Cayce's counsel in all three crucial areas of human challenge. In fact, the initial paragraph of the opening discourse emphasizes the importance of seeing the interconnectedness of all life experiences: ". . . as experiences of the entity throughout the activities in the earth, are one; and must be construed as such—if there will be the proper interpretation of same."

Following that statement, the reading makes an introductory comment about the nature of mind and the origin of challenges from this level. It points out that one's attitudes and emotions are largely influenced by patterns built in two places. First, there are tendencies of emotion which come from previous experiences in the earth plane (i.e., past lives). Second, there are influences more of an attitudinal, mental, or even intuitive flavor that often arise from experiences between earthly lives—what the Cayce readings call "interplanetary sojourns" or, in the case of this reading, "astrological aspects."

At other points in reading 1215-4 there are further references to the mind plus more specific information given to the young man on particular emotional and attitudinal challenges. But it is not the focus of this commentary to pursue those items. Instead, we shall look carefully at the topic emphasized throughout this reading: the challenges faced by this individual to awaken his will and to use it in a way that would lead to soul growth.

The opening discourse continues, following these initial references to the oneness of spirit and the patterns of mind, by featuring the will as a central issue for this particular soul's development. The first point made is that there is a fundamental polarity created by the soul setting its will apart from God's will. We can think in terms of God's intention or God's will in contrast to "self-will," understood as the individual soul's will operating from a limited (or even sometimes rebellious) perspective of life. The reading says this:

> **For God hath not willed that any soul should perish but has prepared with each temptation, each self-willed activity, a way, a manner, a means of escape.**

In other words, this individual (1215)—and indeed all of us—have had experiences in which we used our will's birthright to create a very limited and distorted sense of our own identity. The will is that which gives each of us a feeling of our own unique individuality and goes even further to shape our momentary sense of who we are. Attitudes, emotions, and behaviors which have arisen from moments when our sense of identity was quite limited create a problem for us. Such "self-willed activities" give rise to temptations, and we overcome the temptation only by realigning personal will with God's will (i.e., gaining the sense of our individual identity which matches God's way of knowing us).

The subtlety of the will's role in all of this should not cause us to miss its significance. It is easier to think of our lives merely in terms of the principle "Mind is the builder." But to do so is to miss half the picture of the soul's evolutionary journey. It seems simpler to say, "In the past I have used my mind to build karmic patterns and now I must use my mind aright to undo those distorted soul memories." While such a teaching has in it a measure of truth, it does not instruct us in how to make such a transformation.

Why did the Cayce reading for this 17-year-old present the notion of temptations to be met in terms of the human will? What is it about the will that makes it the key to changing our lives? Simply put, it is this: Unless I have a new sense of my individual identity, efforts at different attitudes, emotions, and behaviors will merely be repressing and not transforming my old ones. It is only in awakening the will that a new sense of who I am can emerge.

The reading for [1215] describes the two primary directions in which the will can take us. One way is toward being a conscious factor in the body of God. The other direction is toward an isolated sense of personal identity in which all of our experiences are self-oriented.

**For with it (the will) one becomes a coordinant, cooperative factor with Creative Forces we know as God, or else becomes self-indulgent, self-glorifying, self-exalting, or makes for those influences that are as karmic forces to be met in the experience of every soul.**

Although the first of these two options is clearly the one which the reading recommends, there is still a natural uncomfortableness which we feel with it. The notion of surrendering our own will to be obedient to God's will does not sit right with something inside us. Is that "something" merely the ego which wants to have its own way? Or is that "something" a wise knowing within us which intuits that nothing really has to be surrendered—it only looks that way from the distorted perspective of the ego?

Perhaps this line of questioning provides a clue for reconciling the polar tension described in the quote above. We all have trouble resolving that tension, but not from a lack of awareness about which option sounds like the best one to take. The problem with the first option (turn my life over to God's will) is that we sense that this somehow violates the integrity of our own individuality, which surely we must retain if there is to be a spiritual quest. The problem with the second option (use my will to get what I want) is that it invariably leads to dissatisfaction and unfulfillment.

The key lies in discovering that there is a "Real Will" of my own soul, of my own unique individuality—and that "Real Will" is harmonious with God's will. I can follow God's will and at the same time have the sense that I am doing exactly what I want to be doing. Or, put another way, it is possible to discover that what my real identity wants for me in life is exactly what God has intended for me.

It is toward such a realization that the source of the Cayce readings is trying to lead (1215). The entire discourse and question/answer exchange can be viewed as counsel which is largely focused upon (1215) properly awakening and using his will to find fulfillment in life. The reading is leading him toward his real identity as a soul—a point from which there shall no longer seem to be an artificial distinction between what the self wills and what God wills.

Two qualities are described as the key for such an awakening by (1215)—perhaps by us all. The first is patience.

> **One open in its manner, with a great imagination; though often self-willed in its choice, and becoming very set in ideas and in giving expression of those influences that create same. Yet the very natures may make for that as becomes in this experience that may be termed the saving grace—*patience*. For in patience, as He hath given, you become aware of your soul.**

In this regard, becoming "aware of your soul" does not mean an intellectual admission that "yes, I probably have a soul." It is, instead, the profound experiencing of one's identity as being a soul. It is a matter of recognizing a new sense of one's own individuality—something that can be born only as an activity of the human will. In other words, patience, the quality that gives us soul-identity and awakens us to our real individuality, is integrally tied in with the will. In fact, in the teaching of Gurdjieff (a Russian contemporary of Cayce, whose ideas often parallel the readings) "patience is the mother of will."

The second quality which is a key for the awakening of will by (1215) (and probably for all of us) is optimism. The reading puts it this way:

> **Hence, the optimism of the entity . . . may bring that consciousness of the purposes for which the entity has entered into the experience.**

What is it about the quality of optimism that is so crucial? A bit later in the reading, we see that, in the course of describing a past-life influence from the American Revolution, the quality is described in terms of "the abilities to make the best of bad situations, the abilities to use that in hand." What happens to us when we are optimistic that makes this quality both an awakener of the will and the revealer of the purpose for our lives?

The key to understanding this matter lies with a principle often repeated in the Cayce readings, although not presented in this particular reading: The mind and the will are in direct opposition to each other. In other words, influences and impressions coming to me from my mind tend to create in me a particular feeling about life and a particular sense of my own identity. Suppose, for example, that I have just become physically sick and on the same day read in the newspaper that stocks in which I have heavily invested have just lost 40% of their value. My mind brings to my awareness many impressions regarding these events. It presents the images of the words in the newspaper and the mental feelings of outrage and disppointment from the financial news. The sense of my own identity which arises from these influences of mind is one of being victimized and downtrodden.

However, to the extent that my will is awakened, I need not settle for this sense of who I am. Recall the principle: The mind and the will are in direct opposition to each other. My will can create a different sense of who I am and of the purposes for my current troublesome experiences. Optimism frees me from the trap I am otherwise caught in if I follow only mental impressions. The ability "to make the best of bad situations" is an act of optimism and will which can transform my sense of purpose in life. It was to such an effort that the source of the Cayce readings seems to be calling (1215).

The reading goes on to promise that no dilemma or troublesome situation is so potent that it could keep the soul from aligning its will with God's and becoming free. Admittedly, there are many patterns of mind stored within us which are out of harmony with universal law. We are continually meeting in daily life the challenges and problems created by such "karmic" patterns of mind. (". . . we may find that the experiences are then such as one meets self continuously . . .") Nevertheless, we always have the option to have our lives directed by will instead of by the old habits of mind. We always have the option to reawaken a different sense of our own identity and to remember that God is present with us and we are part of the Whole.

**For no soul hath wandered so far that when it calls**

**He will not hear. For as the psalmist has given, "Though I take the wings of morning and fly to the utmost parts of the earth, He is there. Though I ascend into heaven, He is there. Though I make my bed in hell, He is there."**

**Hence the purposes for each soul's experience in materiality are that the book of remembrance may be opened (and) that the soul may know its relationship to its Maker.**

**Thus we find, as in this entity's experiences, those influences that bring again, again, again, the opportunity to know the Lord, that He *is* good.**

Then, with the conclusion of this initial discourse of reading 1215-4, the topic shifts first to astrological influences (in which the impact of several planets is discussed) and then to past-life influences.

Four past lifetimes are described. In the third past-life scenario the setting is ancient Persia. From here there come soul memories related to particular influences that could bring healing once again into his life. And there were writing talents that could be reclaimed in this lifetime. In the fourth past-life scenario the setting is prehistoric Atlantis. From here there are talents and experiences regarding "tales as of travel, the activities that have to do with strange lands, strange people, strange customs . . ." Apparently reinvolving himself with these themes and using talents of communications developed then could have a strong impact on the current lifetime.

However, it is the first and second past-life scenarios that seem particularly relevant to the theme of the initial discourse: awakening and aligning the will. In the first past-life scenario, the setting is the American Revolution and (1215) is a leader of what the reading implies are colonial resistance forces at the battle of Bunker Hill.

It was here that the entity demonstrated a development of the will to bring harmony and strength among the team which he led. Stimulated by his will, he experienced an awakening of a sense of "purposeful service." What made such an activity of will a developmental progression for the soul was the lack of self-glory in the activity.

**The entity gained; for through the experience— while the will, the dominant factor, made for personal activities and gain—these were used not for self-indulgence nor for self-glory; and though the**

**body suffered in the material things, in the mental and in the spiritual gains were made.**

In the second past-life scenario the setting is the Roman Empire in a time when early Christians are being persecuted. As a Roman soldier, (1215) "saw suffering, and the entity made light of same." Through the laws of karma, "the entity sees suffering in self" in the present lifetime. How is he now to react? The natural tendency of his mind might be to feel sorry for himself or to be angry at the apparent sources of his suffering. But instead an act of will is recommended. He must learn to "make light" of his own suffering as he did that of others in the past. But this time the motivation—the purpose—which directs his making light of suffering shall be different than in the past. It shall be out of his current sensitivity to the grace of God and not out of his insensitivity to the plight of others.

The reading concludes with a series of questions and answers, none of which is more direct and immediately relevant to the overall themes of the reading than is this fifth one. It links power and love and purpose to the expression of the human will. The parents have posed the question to Cayce:

> **Q-5. How much should we expect of him?**
> **A-5. All! Expect all! As all life, all force, all power, all love is God—then there is a purpose, there is the expression of the will. Then keep it in that.**

# Reading Number 1215-4 _____

*This psychic reading given by Edgar Cayce at his home on Arctic Crescent, Virginia Beach, Va., this 4th day of June, 1937 . . .*

Mr. Cayce: (In going back over years to birth date— "1934—Change—'30 another. Change—") Yes, we have the records here of that entity now known as or called (1215).

In giving the interpretation of this record, as we find, these as conditions, as experiences of the entity throughout the activities in the earth, are one; and must be construed as such—if there will be the proper interpretation of same.

For the activities in the earth become as the emotional influences in the experience of an entity in any sojourn; while the environs about the earth—or those termed astrological aspects—become as the innate influences, or those that are oft expressed intuitively, or from the unseen forces of the influence—hence oft, as they have been interpreted by many, become ruling forces.

But as we find there is no greater influence than the will of an entity, that which is indeed the birthright to each soul. For with it (the will) one becomes a coordinant, cooperative factor with Creative Forces we know as God, or else becomes self-indulgent, self-glorifying, self-exalting, or makes for those influences that are as karmic forces to be met in the experience of every soul.

For God hath not willed that any soul should perish but has prepared with each temptation, each self-willed activity, a way, a manner, a means of escape. Hence we find, in giving those forces that may be helpful influences in the experience of this entity, in the present:

It is well to understand that these are given as that which may be weighed in the balance, and then applied in the choice for constructive experience towards the will, the desire of that Creative Force, or God. From the astrological sojourns and the combination of the experiences in the earth, we find these as outstanding forces in the mien or manner of expression of the entity:

One open in its manner, with a great imagination; though often self-willed in its choice, and becoming very set in ideas and in giving expression of those influences that create same. Yet the very natures may make that as becomes in this experience what may be termed the saving grace— *patience.* For in patience, as He hath given, you become aware of your soul.

Hence the optimism of the entity, its faith—in self, in self-will, guided, directed in making same as one with the Creative Forces—may bring that consciousness of the purposes for which the entity has entered into the experience. And from those premises that He hath not willed that any soul should perish, we may find that the experiences are then such as one meets self continuously in

124

the choices that have been made throughout the experiences in the material plane. Though one may make for that as may be self-willed, there is the advocate in Him, in that "Believe—ask—and ye shall receive." For no soul hath wandered so far that when it calls He will not hear. For as the psalmist has given, "Though I take the wings of the morning and fly to the utmost parts of the earth, He is there. Though I ascend into heaven, He is there. Though I make my bed in hell, He is there." Hence the purposes for each soul's experience in materiality are that the book of remembrance may be opened (and) that the soul may know its relationship to its Maker. Thus we find, as in this entity's experiences, those influences that bring again, again, again, the opportunity to know the Lord, that He *is* good.

In the astrological aspects we find these as the greater ruling influences in the entity: Jupiter is in the benevolent aspects, while the influences of Neptune with Saturn are in the opposite aspects. Hence those forces for sudden change that have had, do have to do with water, with the aspects of the elemental forces, become a part of the entity innately. Hence the intuitive forces in the experiences of the entity.

In Venus we find a benevolent influence. Hence as is indicated, love, patience, brotherly love, gentleness become necessary forces in the material aspects of the entity in the present sojourn; and these need to be such as to overcome that which has been gained by activities in those forces that have brought and do bring about the opposite force for the soul's reaction.

As to the sojourns in the earth, we find these—while varying in their aspects—are rather definite in their influence in the present experience or sojourn; and are a part of the whole, as has been indicated:

Before this (that makes for an activity in the present) the entity was in the earth during that period when there were changes in the affairs of the entity through what is now known as or called the American Revolution; when there were those activities in and about Bunker Hill. The entity then, as one Patrick Pitcairn, was active as a leader, as one that offered resistances, that made for a union of activities when there were those forces that apparently would overshadow. Yet through the very *will* of the entity, and by the force and power of its personality, it brought harmony among its associates and greater strength and determinations in their activities for resistances to that which to each was a purposeful service, a purposeful giving in activities during those experiences and trying times. The entity gained; for through the experience—while the will, the dominant factor, made for personal activities and gain—these were used not for self-indulgence nor for self-glory; and though the body suffered in the material things, in the mental and in the spiritual gains were made.

In the present there is that characteristic of orderliness, of cheeriness; and there are the abilities to make the best of bad situations, the abilities to use that in hand. And would that every soul would learn that lesson, even as well as this entity has gained in the present!

Before that we find the sojourn that is the more outstanding, as to the influences in the present. It was during those periods when there were the persecutions of those who followed in the way of the teachings of the Nazarene. The entity then was a Roman soldier, and one given rather to that of self-indulgence—and glorified rather in seeing the suffering of those who held to that principle. And the entity fought in the arena and watched many that had met the entity fight again with the beasts and with those elements that made for the closer association with the elementals in the sojourn. The entity saw suffering, and the entity made light of same. Hence the entity sees suffering in self in the present, and must again make light of same—but for a different purpose, for a different desire, for a different cause.

For again the entity meets self in that wished, that desired on the part of those against whom the entity held grudges. Hence the entity may find in the present that, in the application of those influences that arose in that period when the entity—known as Claudiusen—brought disturbances in the minds of those with a purpose, that purposefulness must arise within self in the present for meeting those very forces. And only in Him who *is* life, light and immortality, against whom the entity then sought reactions in the material, may same be met; and it must be as has been given: "Make the paths straight, for straight is the way and narrow is the gate by which the understanding and the wisdom of the use of power, force, mercy or truth may be applied in the experience of a soul in the material plane."

Before that we find the entity was in the "city in the hills and the plains," or the Persian or Arabian land. The entity then was among the Grecians who came into the land for the persecutions, for overriding same; but meeting with the leader in the experience, being healed from an injury then by those activities, there came a change in the entity's purposes, the entity's aims, the entity's desires. These then again may be a part of the entity's experience, if there will be made the closer walk with the Creative Forces in the activities of the mental, the material, the spiritual.

For first in spirit, then in mind the builder, may there come—even as then—the healing forces for the entity through the applications of that which *is* the healing power in mechanical means, in the spirit, or in the chemical and in the elementals or the vapors that become a part of every experience before it becomes a manifested form. For first the seed, then the awakening, and then the movement, and then the activity, and then doth the blade appear. Then doth the stalk and the ear shoot forth. So with man in his seeking, as the entity gained in those experiences there—in the name then Esdrel. In the present from that experience may come the activities wherein the entity may gain much by those associations as gained in that sojourn, that activity; and the abilities as the scribe, as the writer, as those activities that may bring the influence for purposes in the earth, may arise in the experience.

Before that we find the entity was in the Atlantean land, during those periods when there were the beginnings of the exodus owing to the destructive forces that had been begun by the sons of Belial. The entity was among the princes of the land that made for the separating of those influences wherein there might be established the journeyings to other lands, with the keepings of records, with the permanent establishments of activities that have become a part of that ye call civilization in the present time.

Hence we find the entity making for the establishments in the Yucatan, in the Luzon, in what became the Inca, in the North American land, and in what later became the land of the Mound Builders in Ohio; also the establishments of those activities in the upper portion of what is now the eastern portion of the land. The entity then was not only one skilled in aircraft and in watercraft, as an aviator and a navigator, but made great strides in keeping in touch with other lands through the forces of nature in the experience.

Hence those things of nature that have to do with communications become a part of the entity's experience. The imaginations of tales as of travel, the activities that have to do with strange lands, strange people, strange customs, become as a portion of the innate forces. And from those very influences may there arise later in this experience those activities that may bring again renown to the entity in this experience. Then the name was Ex-Cex.

As to the abilities of the entity in the present, then, and that to which it may gain or attain, and how: Study to show thyself, first, approved unto Him who doeth *all things* well. Know in *whom,* as well as in what, ye have believed; knowing that in truth and in life and in Him there *is* the sufficient to keep thee and thy desire, thy purposes as one with His. Kick not against the pricks but *love* good, love honor, love patience. For divine love may bring the knowledge, the understanding, the wisdom for the activities to bring the self in accord with Creative Forces.

In the applying of self in the field of art, of literature, of things as pertain to communications, become a part of the entity's experience. In these we may find material gains. Let the love of the fellow man and the love of God be one. Ready for questions.

**Q-1.** *What is his life expectancy?*

**A-1.** This depends upon the application of that which is a part of the experience in the present. It should be many, many, many moons.

**Q-2.** *What can he take up in the immediate future?*

**A-2.** Composition and storytelling, story writing and the like—that deal with communications in strange experiences, strange places, strange surroundings.

**Q-3.** *What preparation should he have for his life work, and should it be pushed at the present time?*

**A-3.** It should be rather a part of the whole development, than pushed. Let it be rather an *unfoldment* in the experiences for the activities that make the desire and the will to be independent in its activities; that is, as this:

There is the expression of what is expected to do, to be

done. Then let this be carried forward in the means and manners of preparation in self for the ability to unfold in these directions.

**Q-4.** *How far will his strength allow him to go?*

**A-4.** He may be a blessing to many. Do not count as man in multitudes but rather as God that looketh on the purposes and the desires of the individual soul, to make self as helpful, as hopeful to others, that they, too, may see the light—and the way.

**Q-5.** *How much should we expect of him?*

**A-5.** All! Expect all! As all life, all force, all power, all love is God—then there is a purpose, there is the expression of the will. Then keep it in that. For what ye expect, and ask for, that ye see, that ye experience.

**Q-6.** *Would it be wise to take him south next winter?*

**A-6.** This depends to be sure much upon the developments. But as we find, all considered in the present—for there will be much change, especially in the use of the upper portion of self—would be well.

**Q-7.** *How develop more worthwhile friendships?*

**A-7.** Through the abilities in self to supply interests for others in the very activities of the mental self in the present. For that in which one is interested, one finds the interest in others; and this develops a bond of sympathy, a bond of love, a bond of friendship; and is a growing thing.

**Q-8.** *What advice to his parents in regard to his best development?*

**A-8.** Keep optimistic; keep in patience; keep in love.

For there is committed to thy care a great soul that may give much to others that they, too, may find hope when *materially* the earth and the things therein look dark. Let the light of love in, then, to the heart that is seeking the love of the Christ. We are through for the present.

1215-4

# THE SLEEPING TALENT

*by Henry Reed, Ph.D.*

If there is any one truth from the legacy of the Cayce readings that would be the most important to remember, it would be that there is a spiritual dimension to human beings, something beyond time and space boundaries. Another way of expressing this is to say that all human beings are interconnected, one with all other elements in creation. This spiritual oneness may be perceived not by the senses, which respond to events in the space/time materialized world, but by the faculty of intuition. We each have available a "sixth sense" that is attuned to the oneness dimension in life, providing a means for us to guide our lives in accord with our ideals. Since this sixth sense is so critical a faculty—able to perceive directly the reality of Cayce's emphasis on the spiritual oneness of all life—it is reasonable to ask, "Just where can I find this sixth sense of mine?" To such a question, Cayce might reply, with a twinkle in his eye, "Well, you're sleeping on it."

Such an answer is a good joke, because it's really true. It's true in that the talent is dormant, asleep. It's true also in that sense suggested, "You're sitting on it . . . it's closer than you think, but you are hiding it from yourself." And it's also true in the sense that during sleep the talent of the sixth sense becomes most active, aware, or awake.

How can something be awake when we are asleep? That seems like a contradiction. But consider the story of Edgar Cayce himself, for his life gives credence to our tongue-in-cheek answer to the location of the sixth sense. Edgar Cayce was called "the sleeping prophet." Here was a man who very often was "asleep on the job." Did you know that he first discovered his talent for clairvoyance in his sleep? So Cayce would be speaking from direct experience should he answer our question concerning the location of our sixth sense by saying, "You're sleeping on it."

Since such a profound fact seems camouflaged in such an ordinary event—sleep—it is no wonder that, at some point, Edgar Cayce was specifically asked about this common mystery. In fact, in 1932 the sleeping prophet was asked to explain about the nature of sleep. This question resulted in a series of three readings numbered 5754, the first two of which are considered here. It was not a reading for a particular individual, but rather Edgar Cayce was asked to give a clear and comprehensive outline of what happens in sleep, a presentation that could be made available to the general public. So what Cayce answered in response to this question was meant for you and me to hear.

To put yourself in the mood for appreciating the answer, imagine first the extraordinary situation that is occurring— extraordinary, that is, from our usual viewpoint. It is easy to imagine someone about to depart to a foreign country, and our asking our friend to send us a postcard letting us know what it's like over there. But can you imagine lying down to go to sleep and having someone at your bedside ask you, "When you get to sleep, please tell me what it's like." That's what was being asked of Edgar Cayce.

Reflect for a moment . . . what is it like to fall asleep? What happens? Where do we go? Why don't we remember? Since childhood most of us have at some point wondered about the mystery of sleep. We know that we lie down, our body relaxes, and we think about this and that as we "drift off." Sometimes something disturbs us just as we fall asleep, and these occasions show us that right before we were awakened, we were so caught up in what we were thinking about that we had lost awareness of our surroundings and had just about taken our thoughts for our reality. That much about sleep we have observed for ourselves. But not much more. When we awaken hours later, we cannot account for the time spent. We simply don't remember. It feels as if we had "blanked out." About the only evidence we have of experiences while we were asleep is when we happen to remember a dream. Or perhaps we awaken in a particularly striking mood which makes us wonder what might have triggered such a feeling state.

Just what does happen while we are asleep? The answer

to this question in the reading begins by commenting upon our common-sense approach to researching sleep—that is, our science of studying the residues of sleep—dreams—in order to form ideas or theories about how such residues may have been created. The reading is saying that such an approach may help prove one psychoanalyst's theory over that of another theorist, but that it won't tell us much about what is really happening during sleep.

To appreciate the significance of this criticism of then-current sleep research and Cayce's amazing ability to predict what later scientific research would finally discover, consider for a moment the state of the art of sleep and dream research at the time of this reading. Freud had published his groundbreaking book, *The Interpretation of Dreams,* 30 years before, in 1900. It introduced the notion that there existed certain predictable and identifiable processes by which dreams were formed, psychological defense mechanisms that created symbolism out of mental residues arising during sleep. The process was thought to resemble the process of insanity. Freud's theory prompted many experiments of the sort Cayce is criticizing. For example, a common type of experiment was exposing someone to an upsetting experience prior to going to sleep, or to disturbing physical sensations while the person slept. The person's dreams would then be examined to see how the upsetting experience may have been symbolized in the dream. But it wasn't until 30 years after Cayce gave this reading that laboratory scientists discovered that dreaming is a natural biological process, occurring in timely cycles during the night. And now, over 50 years after this reading, sleep scientists are discovering what Cayce described for us—that the mind never sleeps.

This first reading, 5754-1, describes sleep as a "shadow of, that intermission in earth's experiences of, that state called death ..." It is like death in two respects: first, because the physical aspect of consciousness becomes unaware of physical conditions surrounding the body; and second, because there awakens a larger awareness that transcends time and space, an awareness available after death.

The reading discusses the nature of awareness itself and its relation to the senses. How do you know, right now, that you are aware of being aware, or conscious? Isn't it because you can refer to information that your senses are providing you? "I know that I am aware because I see things, hear things, and feel things." When falling asleep, this reading points out, we become less aware, in that the senses we normally use to remind us of our awareness are shutting down. This shutting down corresponds to that experience we have all had, mentioned earlier, when a loud noise, for example, breaks into our drifting off to sleep and we realize that we were about to fall asleep. Or when someone is reading to us, and we realize we must have drifted off to sleep because we are suddenly aware that we haven't been hearing what was being said.

The reading qualifies this statement about the senses shutting down by pointing out that they do so to the extent necessary to remain on guard for the protection of the sleeping person. It is as if we keep "an ear cocked," as the expression goes, remaining slightly on guard in case some event should happen that would require us to awaken and take action.

The physical consciousness is shutting down its response to *physical* information (except for what is needed for protection) but is *not* shutting out information from the imagination or from unconscious processes. That we are still aware of our imagination and of unconscious processes is another aspect of the reading's assertion that sleep is like death, for in both states do we interact with these dimensions. It is also pointing ahead to the process of dream formation, as we shall see. For the purposes of an explanation to the general public, the reading is attempting to describe separately processes that must be understood as happening simultaneously and interactively. Describing the process of falling asleep as one in which the awareness based on physical sensations becomes dimmed, the reading singles out the sense of hearing, but not simply in terms of our "keeping an ear cocked" as we fall asleep. In describing the effects in the *body* as we fall asleep, the auditory sense is discussed as being "subdivided" into all the other senses! What could that mean?

"Listen to what your body is trying to tell you!" Have you ever heard that advice? It is a suggestion to pay attention to subtle clues from your body so as to become more cooperative with its natural mode of operation. The suggestion makes sense, but why do we say "listen" rather than "look"? There is something very basic to the sense of listening. The reading terms it the more "universal" of the senses, the first to develop in the evolutionary process. In human beings, at least, the sense of hearing is the only one that operates totally from vibrations, without the necessity of other physical or chemical reactions to help receive the sensations. Perhaps it is the pure vibrational quality of hearing that makes it the more universal sense.

The reading goes on to describe how we "listen" to our body while we sleep. Much of the physical body is at rest during sleep, yet there remain other functions of the body that continue to operate—the heart, the digestion, the breath. How the body maintains the regulation of its physical functioning is still being researched by science. Is this Cayce reading suggesting that the auditory sense plays a role? It does say that the senses act not just through the brain, but through the lymph centers and throughout the sympathetic nervous system. Given our lack of understanding and our bias toward assuming that we think just with our brains, this comment may seem bizarre. However, try to attune to what is being described; imagine a process in which awareness is becoming less active and localized in the brain and becoming more active and diffused throughout the entire body. This awareness during sleep the reading would have us imagine as being like "listening."

It is a listening, however, with the "third ear," for the Cayce source refers to it as "this sixth sense." It calls this awareness that awakens as we fall asleep the sixth sense— both because it is a manner of sensing and because our general use of the term, "the sixth sense," as referring to intuition or ESP is a good approximation to the nature of the ability the reading wishes us to understand.

"Of what, then, does this sixth sense partake . . .?" According to this reading, it depends upon the activities, and the stage is set for us to consider two groups of activities—the activities of our daily life and the activities of our spiritual self. Throughout the rest of the two readings appear references to *comparisons* between these two sets of activities. For the moment, however, this reading mentions that *dreams* are one of the experiences of this sixth sense. Dreams, then, are a function of "listening" with the sixth sense. Listening to what? To the body, at least (but more, for sure) so that through dreams we hear about the condition of our body and can be warned about any impending difficulty.

The sixth sense also "partakes of the *accompanying* entity that is ever on guard before the throne of the Creator itself." Here the reading is now specifically linking sleep, the sixth sense, the spiritual self, and oneness with the Creator. The fact of our spiritual being—here it is that we sleep on it! And it "may be trained or submerged," implying—as the word "sleeper" suggests—that the dormancy of the ability is dependent upon our attitudes and actions toward it; yet, though dormant, it is nevertheless active. The reading goes on to say that it may make itself known to us through disease or depression. Why would a spiritual process manifest itself to us in such a negative manner? The question isn't answered until the second part of the reading. Although it is not explained here the "why" of that effect, the reading does conclude this section by explaining the "how."

It describes the brain as capable of resonance, like "a string tuned that vibrates to certain sound." Recall that during sleep, the senses all, and especially the sixth sense, function as an auditory—that is, vibratory—process. It is stated again, specifically to explain the mechanism of effect that the sleep experiences have upon the waking self: ". . . there is a *definite* connection between that we have chosen to term the sixth sense, or acting through the auditory forces of the body-physical, and the other self within self." What we "hear" while we are asleep continues to resonate with us upon awakening. And since the reading has focused primarily on the physical effects, it concludes by noting that what we make our body with—what we eat—will have an impact on the nature of that resonance.

The majority of the information given in the next reading, 5754-2, pertains to the nature of this awakening sense that for most of us is dormant except when we are asleep. What is particularly exciting about the concepts being explained here is that it suggests to us an alternative awareness, an alternative self, in fact, that lives within us, which is most active during sleep. The nature of this "sleeping talent" is explained in terms of the relationship of sensing to awareness, in terms of the "self" that is aware of sensing, and in terms of what is sensed.

**. . . we find this has been termed, that this ability or this functioning—that is so active when physical consciousness is laid aside—or, as has been termed by some poet, when the body rests in the arms of Morpheus—is nearer possibly to that as may be understandable by or to many; for, as given, this activity—as is seen—of a mind, or an attribute of the mind in physical activity—*leaves* a *definite* impression.**

Just as information in the physical world leaves an impression on our physical senses, so does information in the nonphysical world leave an impression on this sixth sense while we are asleep. All during the night this sixth sense is receiving impressions. Some of these impressions are recalled as dreams. More generally, what happens while we sleep is that this sixth sense has access to *all* experiences ever had by the soul in its various incarnations and other sojourns, as well as to the daily experiences of the current personality.

There is a comparison made during sleep of the person's daily life with all that the person's soul has ever experienced and evaluations are made. This comparison of the particulars of a day's life with the overall perspective of several lifetimes is somewhat like the comparison parents make when responding to an event in the life of their child— the child's perspective seems particularly ironic, poignant, sad, or hopeful from the wider perspective of the adult who has a lot more experience to provide a context for evaluating that particular experience. When we awaken from sleep in a particularly good mood or in a particularly bad mood, it is the result of such a comparison having been made. But *who* is doing all this comparing? It is being done via the ability of the sixth sense, but just who is using this ability?

**The activity, or this sixth sense activity, is the activating power or force of the other self. What other self? That which has been builded by the entity or body, or soul, through its experiences as a whole in the material and cosmic world, see? or is as a faculty of the soul-body itself. Hence, as the illustration given, does the subconscious make aware to this active force when the body is at rest, or this sixth sense, some action on the part of self or another that is in disagreement with that which has been builded by that other self, then *this* is the warring of**

**conditions or emotions within an individual.**

This process of making the comparisons, by the way, becomes the clue to the approach recommended in the readings to the interpretation of dreams that are remembered from sleep. For those dreams are the impressions left of making such comparisons between the recent actions of the person and the ideals formed on the basis of many lifetimes.

When considering the subject of ideals formed over many lifetimes, the Cayce source is naturally moved to reflect upon certain of those ultimate, universal and timeless ideals as expressed by the Son—the Master. We are reminded of certain attributes—peace, the silence, harmony, trust, patience, love, joy, and kindness—the fruits of the spirit that are very likely to have become in some way related to the ideals formed over many lifetimes and thus likely to be used by a person in sleep as a criterion for comparison with the experiences during the day.

Here is where the reading answers the question of why our spiritual nature might manifest itself to us in the morning as a negative mood, or as in disease. Having formed over many lifetimes an ideal such as love or peace, when we compare during sleep this ideal (and our related understanding) to our activities and experiences from the day, we ache, we mourn, we yearn that we could but remember what we know! Like the functioning of a thermostat, such feelings of depression are the echoes of the call of the spiritual self, the residue of the tension we have experienced during sleep, attempting to pull us back to the mark. Then, in its remarks on the Son—"He sleeps"—the reading asks us to ponder the parallels between the Death and Resurrection and our own sleeping soul self.

The reading says that this other self has been given names, depending primarily on the function under consideration—soul, soul body, cosmic body, spirit body, dream body, etc.—but that what is really important to understand is that it is an awareness within us that is part of a universal awareness—we are sleeping giants!

The real sleeper in this reading is that in one of the most ordinary of all experiences, sleep, we actually enter into the oneness via universal awareness. If we would only ponder the relation between awareness and the senses, we could wake up within our sleep. For just as our awareness during the day is often hidden from us by being totally reflected by the sensory information given to it, so also at night is that other self reflected in the information coming through the sixth sense, which is also termed intuition.

**How received woman her awareness? Through the sleep of the man! Hence *intuition* is an attribute of that made aware through the suppression of those forces from that from which it sprang, yet endowed *with* all of those abilities and forces of its Maker that made for same its activity in an *aware* world, or—if we choose to term it such—a three-dimensional world, a *material* world, where its beings must see a materialization to become aware of its existence in that plane; yet all are aware that the essence of Life itself—as the air that is breathed—carries those elements that are *not* aware consciously of any existence to the body, yet the body subsists, lives upon such . . .**

**What, then, is the sixth sense . . . the very force or activity of the soul in its experience through *whatever* has been the experience of that soul itself.**

Thus the sixth sense, as depicted so forcefully for us here, is not an appendage, like the ears or the nose, but rather something very central, at the core of our experiences— almost to say that it is what makes *experiences* out of events. It is as if the intuitive sense acting through the soul is what makes the raw events into food for the soul.

"What, then, has this to do—you ask—with the subject of Sleep? Sleep—that period when the soul takes stock of that it *has* acted upon during one rest period to another, making or drawing—as it were—the comparisons that make for Life itself in its *essence* . . ." As intuition—the sixth sense—is suppressed during the day, a weariness sets in as we are not operating with all our intelligence. The fatigue draws us to rest and sleep. When we fall asleep, we withdraw our awareness from its hypnotic fascination with physical sensation, thereby enabling us to listen with our now awakening sixth sense. As we abide in sleep, intuitively resonating with the sum of *all* our experiences—this life and beyond—we gain refreshing perspective on our efforts and have another opportunity to remember what we know. What will you do with *your* sleep tonight?

"In sleep all things become possible . . ." the reading reminds us. Of all the possibilities, what would you have? It makes a difference what we choose to experience during sleep. Many of us think of sleep as a change to *get away* from it all. But this reading is informing us that sleep is a chance to *return* to the joys of our spiritual heritage—our universal awareness—and that which we might wish to explore with that endowment.

How can this be used? By applying the principle of "like attracting like." The things that concern us during the day are going to influence what we experience during the night. It is not so much a matter of giving ourselves suggestions or using some special technique upon falling asleep to direct our sleep time to a particular purpose. Rather, how we live during the day, what our affinities, likes, and dislikes are, the goals and ideals we pursue during the day—these will determine what use we will make of our sleeping talent.

# Reading Numbers 5754-1, -2

*These psychic readings given by Edgar Cayce at his home on Arctic Crescent, Virginia Beach, Va., the 14th and 15th days of July, 1932, in accordance with request made by Hugh Lynn Cayce and those present . . .*

*Mrs. Cayce: You will please outline clearly and comprehensively the material which should be presented to the general public in explaining just what occurs in the conscious, subconscious and spiritual forces of an entity while in the state known as sleep. Please answer the questions which will be asked regarding this.*

Mr. Cayce: Yes. While there has been a great deal written and spoken regarding experiences of individuals in that state called sleep, there has only recently been the attempt to control or form any definite idea of what produces conditions in the unconscious, subconscious, or subliminal or subnormal mind, by attempts to produce a character—or to determine that which produces the character—of dreams as had by an individual or entity. Such experiments may determine for some minds questions respecting the claim of some psychiatrist or psychoanalyst and through such experiments refute or determine the value of such in the study of certain character of mental disturbances in individuals; yet little of this may be called true analysis of what happens to the body, either physical, mental, subconscious or spiritual, when it loses itself in such repose. To be sure, there are certain definite conditions that take place respecting the physical, the conscious, and the subconscious, as well as spiritual forces of a body.

So in analyzing such a state for a comprehensive understanding, all things pertaining to these various factors must be considered.

First, we would say, sleep is a shadow of, that intermission in earth's experiences of, that state called death; for the physical consciousness becomes unaware of existent conditions, save as are determined by the attributes of the physical that partake of the attributes of the imaginative or the subconscious and unconscious forces of that same body; that is, in a normal sleep (from the physical stand-point we are reasoning now) the *senses* are on guard, as it were, so that the auditory forces are those that are the more sensitive. The auditory sense being of the attributes or senses that are more universal in aspect, when matter in its evolution has become aware of itself being capable of taking from that about itself to sustain itself in its present state. That is as of the lowest to the highest of animate objects or beings. From the lowest of evolution to the highest, or to man.

So, then, we find that there are left what is ordinarily known as four other attributes that are acting independently and coordinatingly in *awareness* for a physical body to be conscious. These, in the state of sleep or repose, or rest, or exhaustion, or induced by an influence from the outside, have become *unaware* of that which is taking place about the object so resting.

Then, there is the effect that is had upon the body as to what becomes, then, more aware to those attributes of the body that are not aware of that existent about them, or it. The organs that are of that portion known as the inactive, or not necessary for conscious movement, keep right on with their functioning—as the pulsations, the heart beat, the assimilating and excretory system keep right on functioning; yet there are periods during such a rest when even the heart, the circulation, may be said to be at rest. What, then, *is* that that is not in action during such period? That known as the sense of perception as related to the physical brain. Hence it may be truly said, by the analogy of that given, that the auditory sense is subdivided, and there is the act of hearing by feeling, the act of hearing by the sense of smell, the act of hearing by *all* the senses that are independent of the brain centers themselves, but are rather of the lymph centers—or throughout the entire sympathetic system is such an accord as to be *more* aware, *more* acute, even though the body-physical and brain-physical *is* at repose, or *unaware.*

Of what, then, does this sixth sense partake, that has to do so much with the entity's activities by those actions that may be brought about by that passing within the sense *range* of an entity when in repose, that may be called—in their various considerations or phases—experiences of *something* within that entity, as a dream—that may be either in toto to that which is to happen, is happening, or may be only presented in some form that is emblematical—to the body or those that would interpret such.

These, then—or this, then—the sixth sense, as it may be termed for consideration here, partakes of the *accompanying* entity that is ever on guard before the throne of the Creator itself, and is that that may be trained or submerged, or left to its *own* initiative until it makes either war *with* the self in some manner of expression—which must show itself in a material world as in dis-ease, or disease, or temper, or that we call the blues, or the grouches, or any form that may receive either in the waking state or in the sleep state, that has *enabled* the brain in its activity to become so changed or altered as to respond much in the manner as does a string tuned that vibrates to certain sound in the manner in which it is strung or played upon.

Then we find, this sense that governs such is that as may be known as the other self of the entity, or individual. Hence we find there must be some definite line that may be taken by that other self, and much that then has been accorded—or recorded—as to that which may produce certain given effects in the minds or bodies (not the minds, to be sure, for its active forces are upon that outside of that in which the mind, as ordinarily known, or the brain centers themselves, functions), but—as may be seen by all such experimentation, these may be produced—the same effect—upon the same individual, but they do not produce the same effect upon a different individual in the same environment or under the same circumstance. Then, this should lead one to know, to understand, that there is a *definite* connection between that we have chosen to term the sixth sense, or acting through the auditory forces of the body-physical, and the other self within self.

In purely physical, we find in sleep the body is *relaxed*— and there is little or no tautness within same, and those activities that function through the organs that are under the supervision of the subconscious or unconscious self, through the involuntary activities of an organism that has been set in motion by that impulse it has received from its first germ cell force, and its activity by the union *of* those forces that have been impelled or acted upon by that it has fed upon in all its efforts and activities that come, then it may be seen that these may be shown by due consideration— that the same body fed upon *meats,* and for a period—then the same body fed upon only herbs and fruits—would *not* have the same character or activity of the other self in its relationship to that as would be experienced by the other self in its activity through that called the dream self. We are through for the moment—present.                              5754-1

Now, with that as has just been given, that there is an active force within each individual that functions in the manner of a sense when the body-physical is in sleep, repose or rest, we would then outline as to what are the functions of this we have chosen to call a sixth sense. What relation does it bear with the normal physical recognized five senses of a physical-aware body? If these are active, what relation do they bear to this sixth sense?

Many words have been used in attempting to describe what the spiritual entity of a body is, and what relations this spirit or soul bears with or to the active forces within a physical normal body. Some have chosen to call this the cosmic body, and the cosmic body as a sense in the universal consciousness, or that portion of same that is a part of, or that body with which the individual, or man, is clothed in his advent into the material plane.

These are correct in many respects, yet by their very classification, or by calling them by names to designate their faculties or functionings, have been limited in many respects.

But what relation has this sixth sense (as has been termed in this presented) with this *soul* body, this cosmic consciousness? What relation has it with the faculties and functionings of the normal physical mind? Which must be trained? The sixth sense? Or must the body be trained in its other functionings to the dictates of the sixth sense?

In that as presented, we find this has been termed, that this ability or this functioning—that is so active when physical consciousness is laid aside—or, as has been termed by some poet, when the body rests in the arms of Morpheus—is nearer possibly to that as may be under-standable by or to many; for, as given, this activity—as is seen—of a mind, or an attribute of the mind in physical activity—*leaves* a *definite* impression. Upon what? The mental activities of the body, or upon the subconscious portion of the body (which, it has been termed that, it never forgets), upon the spiritual essence of the body, or upon the soul itself? These are questions not statements!

In understanding, then, let's present illustrations as a pattern, that there may be comprehension of that which is being presented:

The activity, or this sixth sense activity, is the activating power or force of the other self. What other self? That which has been builded by the entity or body, or soul, through its experiences as a whole in the material and cosmic world, see? or is as a faculty of the soul-body itself. Hence, as the illustration given, does the subconscious make aware to this active force when the body is at rest, or this sixth sense, some action on the part of self or another that is in disagree-ment with that which has been builded by that other self, then *this* is the warring of conditions or emotions within an individual. Hence we may find that an individual may from sorrow *sleep* and wake with a feeling of elation. What has taken place? We possibly may then understand what we are speaking of. There has been, and ever when the physical consciousness is at rest, the other self communes with the *soul* of the body, see? Or it goes *out* into that realm of experience in the relationships of all experiences of that entity that may have been throughout the *eons* of time, or in correlating *with* that as it, that entity, *has* accepted as its criterion or standard of judgments, or justice, within its sphere of activity.

Hence through such an association in sleep there may have come that peace, that understanding, that is accorded by that which has been correlated through that passage of the selves of a body in sleep. Hence we find the more spiritual-minded individuals are the more easily pacified, at peace, harmony, in normal active state as well as in sleep. Why? They have set before themselves (Now we are speaking of one individual!) that that *is* a criterion that may be wholly relied upon, for that form which an entity or soul sprang is its *concept,* its awareness of, the divine or creative forces within their experience. Hence they that have named the Name of the Son have put their trust in Him. He their standard, their model, their hope, their activity. Hence we see how that the action through such sleep, or such quieting as to enter the silence—what do we mean by entering the silence? Entering the presence of that which *is* the criterion of the selves of an entity!

On the other hand oft we find one may retire with a feeling of elation, or peace, and awaken with a feeling of depression, of aloofness, of being alone, of being without hope, or of fear entering, and the *body-physical* awakes with that depression that manifests itself as of low spirits, as is termed, or of coldness, gooseflesh over the body, in expressions of the forces. What has taken place? A comparison in that "arms of Morpheus," in that silence, in that relationship of the physical self being unaware of those comparisons between the soul and its experiences of that period with the experiences of itself throughout the ages, and the experience may not have been remembered as a dream—but it lives *on*—and on, and must find its expression in the relationships of all it has experienced in whatever sphere of activity it may have found itself. Hence we find oft individual circumstances of where a spiritual-minded individual in the material plane (that is, to outward appearances of individuals so viewing same) suffering oft under pain, sickness, sorrow, and the like. What takes place? The experiences of the soul are meeting that which it has merited, for the clarification for the associations of itself with that whatever has been set as its ideal. If one has set self in array against that of love as manifested by the Creator, in its activity brought into material plane, then there *must* be a continual—continual—*warring* of those elements. By the comparison we may find, then, how it was that, that energy of creation manifested in the Son—by the activities of the Son in the material plane, could say "He sleeps," while to the outward eye it was death; for He *was*—and *is*—and ever will be—Life and Death in one; for as we find ourselves in His presence, that we have builded in the soul makes for that condemnation or that pleasing of the presence of that *in* His presence. So, my son, let thine lights be in Him, for these are the *manners* through which all may come to an understanding of the activities; for, as was given, "I was in the Spirit on the Lord's day." "I was caught up to the seventh heaven. Whether I was in the body or out of the body I cannot tell." What was taking place? The subjugation of the physical attributes in accord and attune with its infinite force as set as its ideal brought to that soul, "Well done, thou good and faithful servant, enter into the joys of thy Lord." "He that would be the greatest among you"—not as the Gentiles, not as the heathen, not as the scribes or Pharisees, but "He that would be the greatest will be the *servant* of all."

What, then, has this to do—you ask—with the subject of Sleep? Sleep—that period when the soul takes stock of that it *has* acted upon during one rest period to another, making or drawing—as it were—the comparisons that make for Life itself in its *essence*, as for harmony, peace, joy, love, long-suffering, patience, brotherly love, kindness—these are the fruits of the Spirit. Hate, harsh words, unkind thoughts, oppressions and the like, these are the fruits of the evil forces, or Satan and the soul either abhors that it has passed, or enters into the joy of its Lord. Hence we see the activities of same. This an *essence* of that which is intuitive in the active forces. Why should this be so in one portion, or one part of a body, rather than another? How received woman her awareness? Through the sleep of the man! Hence *intuition* is an attribute of that made aware through the suppression of those forces from that from which it sprang, yet endowed *with* all of those abilities and forces of its Maker that made for same its activity in an *aware* world, or—if we choose to term it such—a three-dimensional world, a *material* world, where its beings must see a materialization to become aware of its existence in that plane; yet all are aware that the essence of Life itself—as the air that is breathed—carries those elements that are *not* aware consciously of any existence to the body, yet the body subsists, lives upon such. In sleep all things become possible, as one finds self flying through space, lifting, or being chased, or whatnot, by those very things that make for a comparison of that which has been builded by the very soul of the body itself.

What, then, is the sixth sense? Not the soul, not the conscious mind, not the subconscious mind, not intuition alone, not any of those cosmic forces—but the very force or activity of the soul in its experience through *whatever* has been the experience of that soul itself. See? The same as we would say, is the mind of the body the body? No! Is the sixth sense, then, the soul? No! No more than the mind is the body! For the soul is the *body* of, or the spiritual essence of, an entity manifested *in* this material plane. We are through for the present.                    5754-2

# THE SOURCE OF PSYCHIC ABILITY

*by Henry Reed, Ph.D.*

What is the significance of psychic ability? What value does it have? What does it imply about our nature? Is there something that connects all of us together, like an invisible ether? The existence of psychic ability certainly does add another dimension to our perception of the world.

We are now going to be eyewitnesses to history, studying the record of one of those times in parapsychological research when a psychic is asked for information concerning the nature of the phenomena being manifested. It is a particularly fascinating and unique event because it involves *two* psychics, each giving a reading for the other, comparing their different perspectives on their unique psychic talents.

On February 3, 1934, in a private home on Staten Island in New York, two people who were to become internationally renowned psychics met face to face to conduct an experiment. The one was Edgar Cayce, founder of the Association for Research and Enlightenment. The other was Mrs. Eileen Garrett, the famous medium, founder of the Parapsychology Foundation and benefactor of much research into parapsychology. These two gifted psychics came together to conduct readings for one another concerning their psychic talents. Edgar Cayce went first, reading for Mrs. Garrett. The resulting discourse, reading 507-1, is what we present for study here. Mrs. Garrett's reading for Cayce, referred to in our discussion, is recorded as an appendix to reading 507-1 and is available for study in the A.R.E. Library.

Before we examine the results of this unusual experiment, it would be helpful first to consider certain terms and issues within the science of parapsychology as they apply to the psychic manifestations of Edgar Cayce and Eileen Garrett. This background may help us better to appreciate the significance of the material we will study.

Cayce is generally classified by parapsychologists as a "clairvoyant," that term designating the type of psychic ability that he manifested. Clairvoyance can be contrasted with telepathy (another category of psychic ability), which involves the ability of one mind being able to receive or tune in to information that is present in another mind. It is like talking over the telephone, but without the material phone. In telepathy two minds are involved.

Clairvoyance, on the other hand, involves picking up information that is not in anyone else's mind, but is simply "out there." Clairvoyance is knowledge at a distance; knowing from afar without the involvement, either directly or indirectly, of a second, intermediary mind.

Making distinctions between such processes as telepathy and clairvoyance is important to parapsychologists as they attempt to understand how the psychic operates and the implications this has for our nature. Telepathy suggests a particular kind of ability and a certain type of "mental link-up" between people, whereas clairvoyance suggests possibly a different, or additional ability, and adds further possibilities to the makeup of human consciousness and the nature of reality.

While Cayce was characterized as a clairvoyant, Mrs. Garrett was generally described as a medium; that is to say, her psychic information originated from nonmaterial "spirits" who spoke through her. It was as if her entranced consciousness was a radio receiver, picking up transmissions from beings inhabiting another dimension. Cayce, on the other hand, insisted that he was not a medium, that he did not obtain his information through the use of any nonmaterial entities; rather, he claimed that his information came from a clairvoyance that extended as if toward omniscience, tending to make all knowledge available to him. He explained that such extended clairvoyance was possible because every experience ever had by a person since the creation of this planet leaves a "record," a mark on the history book of creation that may be read by others who are properly attuned.

Now we can see some of the issues in parapsychological study that are raised by the comparison of these two psychics. If Cayce is using clairvoyance to tap into knowledge, is Mrs. Garrett using telepathy to communicate with spirits? Who are these spirits, what is their nature, and would communication with nonmaterial minds constitute telepathy, as we might ordinarily think of it, or some other process? Finally, are these two psychics having us make different inferences about the question of the continuity of life? As a medium, Mrs. Garrett seems to draw attention to the continuity *in activity* of physically deceased beings, while as a clairvoyant, Cayce seems to draw attention to the continuity of the *effects,* or of the records left behind. With this background, let us now study the reading that Edgar Cayce gave for Eileen Garrett.

Hugh Lynn Cayce conducted the reading and asked Cayce to speak specifically about Eileen Garrett's mediumship, giving "such information regarding her work which will be interesting and helpful in relation to our experiments today."

The reading begins with an opening statement that lays the foundation for the answers given later.

> **As to that which may be helpful to those that seek to know that there is the continuity of life, that there is to be gained from those activities in the realm of soul forces that may act through the psychic forces in each individual soul, know that that which may be given through this entity is that which is received through the varied channels that present themselves in that atmosphere or that environ that seeks for an understanding in those fields of activity that may bring to the manifested actions of individuals those influences that may have to bear upon the lives and souls of individuals.**

The reading first acknowledges the reasons for being interested in the phenomena being discussed here: You are interested in knowing what help may be gained concerning the question of the continuity of life from the study of information that is transmitted psychically from the activities of soul forces. In other words, what do we really learn about the afterlife by asking psychics? (Note that what is implied is that the general source of the information is "activities in the realm of soul forces," and that such activities then operate "through the psychic forces in each individual . . ." We are reminded of the readings' general principle: Psychic ability should be thought of as an attribute of the soul, rather than, for example, of the mind. What difference that makes we will see later.)

The statement then makes reference to what may be learned from Eileen Garrett ("that which may be given through this entity . . ."). It says that she receives information from "varied channels that present themselves," and they are located not in a physical place (such as the place where would be found those seeking Mrs. Garrett's help), but rather "in that atmosphere or that environ"—a phrase used in other readings when referring to "places" within the nonmaterial dimensions of being. ("Place" here means a "state of being," as when we ask someone, "What kind of place are you in?"; meaning, "How is your mood and what kinds of things are you thinking about?")

What is the quality of the "place" where these varied channels present themselves? Cayce characterizes it as the kind "that seeks for an understanding . . ." What quality of understanding? That which would be an active understanding, bridging the actions of people with the influences of the soul. That is to say, the nature of the "transmission" is governed by the desire to make the soul's influence a more conscious part of the person's daily life.

"As to how" all this works and to what effect, the follow-up remarks indicate that it depends upon the sincerity of purpose of the seeker: "For, as ye sow, so shall ye reap." Here is where it makes a difference that psychic ability is of the soul rather than simply of the mind. We are normally inclined to think in terms of mechanisms and techniques, but the reading indicates it is rather a matter of purpose. The purpose of the seeker rather than, for example, the nature of the trance or of the nonmaterial, guiding entity is what determines the phenomenon. Circumstances and tools are but that, whereas it is the purpose of the one using them that determines what actually results from their use.

Is the seeker someone who is looking for influences to put into constructive action, or is the seeker looking instead for ideas to cram into one's head, puffing it up with fanciful notions? The difference in how the information is to be used affects the type of information that is given.

What a different notion of the psychic forces and their activity do we have here! The reading is suggesting that it is not simply a matter of plugging this particular receiver into this particular source of information using that particular antenna, but rather what the receiver can receive, what source of information will be active, and what information will be given, all depends upon the purpose of the seeker. What you put into the experience determines what you get out of it. The seeker determines the nature of the information just as much as possibly the mechanism by which the psychic obtains that information.

This reading concludes its opening remarks, then, by referring the responsibility for both the generation and the evaluation of such phenomena back to the seeker, rather than to those observers who may be standing by to study the phenomena. It states: ". . . so only self may find those influences through such a channel that will be to meet the needs of those things necessary in self's experience for the greater development."

When the Cayce source is questioned, he is asked first from what source he is getting this information for Mrs. Garrett. The answer is quite simply that it comes from "those records" formed by her activities; in other words, from her herself, as if from the footprints she has left. Here we see Cayce making reference to his ability as a clairvoyant to read the record created by the person's past experience.

When he is asked the source of Mrs. Garrett's information, he answers that it comes from two sources. First, it comes as a result of her own soul development that makes her a channel to others, who are seeking a bridge between the spiritual and psychic forces and their own lives. Second, it comes from "those influences from without that are either in those attitudes of being teachers, instructors, directors, or those that would give to those in the material plane the better comprehension of the continuance of a mental and soul activity." Thus Cayce refers to two distinct sources: Mrs. Garrett's own attunement and the activity of other influences. (Here is a rather explicit reference to something like spirit guides, although again he describes more their intent than their nature.)

Next comes a series of questions concerning the purpose,

development and perfection of Mrs. Garrett's psychic ability. The answer states that the purpose is for self-expression: to express the desire and fulfillment of a soul who has worked at being a channel to the material realm of the knowledge and blessings in the spiritual realm. Her psychic gifts are a natural expression and outgrowth of her purposeful development as a soul endeavoring to be of a particular service. The reading explains that in one past life, for example, Mrs. Garrett served as a spiritual teacher.

Thus her current work as a psychic builds upon past work with the psychic realm, ever with the same theme: to awaken in others the relationship between the unseen and the seen. As to how she might further perfect this ability, the reading doesn't recommend particular techniques, but rather encourages her to continue as before, seeking to remain true to the best and the highest within herself:

> **. . . for, as He has promised ever, if ye seek in the light of thine understanding, trusting in Him for the increase, so may this attitude being kept ever within self make for self being that channel through which only the constructive influences may come into the experience of the seeker.**

Note that the discussion of Mrs. Garrett's psychic ability, its origin, development, and use, is strictly in terms of her purposes, the ideals she served, rather than in terms of any mechanisms short of a central truth of creation that "the Father giveth ever the increase . . ." It seems to want to stress that aspect of psychic ability over mechanics or techniques. As in many of his other readings, Cayce is here, too, implying that we already have within us the ability to learn such talents, if we would simply set our purpose in accord with the purpose of such abilities and then put into application what we do know ("in the light of thine understanding"), and take it from there. Having emphasized this most central aspect of psychic functioning, the reading goes on to answer more specific questions about the mechanisms.

It is especially interesting now to note how Cayce responds to the question concerning the nonmaterial entities involved in Mrs. Garrett's mediumship:

> **Q-6. Who are Mrs. Garrett's spiritual guides, and tell us something about them?**
> **A-6. Let them rather speak for themselves through that channel that is capable rather of presenting**

**them in their light to that which has been the development of the soul itself in its experiences in the earth in the realms of their activity. For, their names are rather in *her* experience, in *her* seeking, than to find through other channels; even though they may be coming from the records that are made by each in their activity. Speak for thyself.**

In not answering this question, the reading makes a number of very fascinating statements. In fact, it may be that it *does* answer the question even if appearing not to. Is it saying that these guides are a reality only to Mrs. Garrett? Not exactly, for it does indicate that their source may be "the records" of their past activity, as if to say that their records might be "there" to be read by Cayce himself. It doesn't explicitly indicate whether or not he could read these records, but we might surmise that he could. The tenor of what is being said seems to suggest that he would rather not, for to do so would give a false or misleading impression of their nature.

It would seem, then, that the significant aspect of their nature lies in the experience of Mrs. Garrett with them. That may be what the reading means when it says that her soul development involved interactions with their activity. If, as is so often suggested and explicitly emphasized in this reading, nothing that a person manifests is separate from what that soul itself has developed, then the spirit guides must be a reflection of Mrs. Garrett's own soul development. Are they reflections, then, of her own past lives, or are they the souls of people with whom she had interacted in past lives? If so, why didn't the reading say something simple like that? It definitely implies that the information which might be produced about these entities from their records would be different from the information Mrs. Garrett would produce by having the spirit guides speak directly: ". . . their names are rather in *her* experience, in *her* seeking . . ."

Let us turn, then, for a moment to see what information came through Mrs. Garrett on this topic. The record of the reading indicates that the source of her information identified itself as "Uvani" and revealed that its last incarnation was at the time of Mohammed. Much of what Uvani stated during this reading supports or complements what Cayce had given. Note Uvani's description of how Cayce obtains his clairvoyant information:

". . . he looks at the description of life in his own experience and by the light of his own spiritual understanding he immediately sees the spirit contact of the personality and what has been given to the soul in experience. After all, there is no example, there is no judge but your own self . . ." (507-1 Supplement)

Sound familiar? Uvani also confirms the existence of the difference between Cayce and Mrs. Garrett that we have referred to as his clairvoyance and her mediumship. In fact, Uvani presents many arguments to the effect that Cayce could function as a better psychic, and with less personal cost, if he were to allow himself to be a medium and take advantage of the entities that wish to speak through him. Uvani presents no information to clarify the nature of such entities although he does make remarks echoing the reading's own statements that they can be identified by their intentions, their desire to help and to make the invisible realms known to the living. When asked to name an entity that was waiting to help Cayce, Uvani gives a reply similar to that reply given by Cayce which we have been pondering. Uvani says, in effect, that it is up to Cayce himself to determine!

What has Cayce determined for himself? In the record of this Cayce reading, he was asked two questions on this matter. First, he was asked that if he "has ever had controls, does he know who they are?" (*control* being a word used to designate the "controlling entity" speaking through the channel). The reply is enigmatic, but of interest: "Anyone may speak who may seek, if the entity or the soul's activities will allow same; or if the desire of the individuals seeking so over commands as to make for a set channel." No particular entity is named, only an indication that this type of communication is possible. The answer sounds like a description of the cooperation of wills, rather than a description of a transmission process. It is the *desire* of the spirit entity that seems to be a strong determining factor.

In the last question asked in ths reading, it is indicated that the information being channeled is "Being directed . . . from the records through Halaliel." Does that mean that Cayce is using a spirit control here? During Mrs. Garrett's reading, Uvani is asked about this and responds in the affirmative, suggesting that this particular entity is very desirous of helping Cayce and should be utilized more. Uvani explains that at times when Cayce is physically tired and drained is it most likely for entities to speak through him, and that it would be better for Cayce if he were to actively choose to seek the help of a particular entity, such as this Halaliel. Edgar Cayce asked about Halaliel in a later reading (262-72) and subsequently chose *not* to seek Halaliel's help.

Returning to reading 507-1, we examine the final section, which consists of a series of questions asked Cayce about his psychic trance. Why does he use hypnosis? The reading answers that his body development is such that in order to seek what is available through the soul-body, the physical body must be put to sleep so that it ceases to influence what is channeled. Asked if trance were then a helpful method for psychic functioning, the Cayce source indicates that there are many methods of manifesting the soul, but that the most important ingredient is the desire to utilize this information in the service of soul development. When asked, is he "clairvoyant in the hypnotic state?" Cayce gives a surprising answer, for he indicates he would be more clairvoyant in the normal waking state, would his body permit of such attunement. It may seem surprising to hear that the normal state of consciousness would be the best state of mind for being psychic, since Cayce himself had to use a trance and so often reminded us that we could most readily experience our psychic ability in the dream state. However, when we consider one of his final remarks, concerning states of consciousness and psychic ability, we may appreciate then what has been an enduring theme throughout this entire reading:

> . . . *all* are one when in perfect accord with the universal forces from which the records of all activities may be taken.

Telepathy implies separation, even the bridging of the separation, a transmission from one person/place to another. Clairvoyance implies a unity, an enlargement of one consciousness to include what would be known. The emphasis on clairvoyance turns our attention away from the problem of how the psychic "bridges the gap" between minds and has us focus on the essential nature of psychic ability, its source in soul activity. Perhaps the most important attribute of the soul is its dwelling in oneness, and it is this oneness that is the significance and source of psychic ability.

# Reading Number 507-1 ——

*This psychic reading given by Edgar Cayce at the home of Mr. and Mrs. . . . N.Y., this 3rd day of February, 1934 . . .*

*Hugh Lynn Cayce: Now you will have before you the soul entity now known as Eileen Garrett, present in this room. You will give at this time such information regarding her work which will be interesting and helpful in relation to our experiments today. You will answer the questions which I will ask.*

Mr. Cayce: Yes, we have the entity, the soul entity, Eileen Garrett, here, present in this room.

As to that which may be helpful to those that seek to know that there is the continuity of life, that there is to be gained from those activities in the realm of soul forces that may act through the psychic forces in each individual soul, know that that which may be given through this entity is that which is received through the varied channels that present themselves in that atmosphere or that environ that seeks for an understanding in those fields of activity that may bring to the manifested actions of individuals those influences that may have to bear upon the lives and souls of individuals.

As to how, to whom, or from what sources these emanations or activities may take their action, depends upon first the sincerity of purpose, as to whether it is to be constructive in the experience of such seekers or whether through self there is to be the aggrandizement of power, influence or force upon and in the experience. For, as ye sow, so shall ye reap.

As there are only those influences in self that may separate the knowledge of the constructive influence in the life; so only self may find those influences through such a channel that will be to meet the needs of those things necessary in self's experience for the greater development.

Ready for questions.

**Q-1.** *Explain how this information is now being given for Mrs. Garrett, the source of this information.*

**A-1.** Being given through that which has been builded in the life and the experience of Mrs. Garrett, and taken from those records made by such activities.

**Q-2.** *What is the source of Mrs. Garrett's psychic information?*

**A-2.** A portion is from the soul development of the entity, that has made and does make for a channel through which spiritual or psychic forces may manifest in a material world; and thus giving that to which the seekers may find in their own particular field of activity. Also from those influences from without that are either in those attitudes of being teachers, instructors, directors, or those that would give to those in the material plane the better comprehension of the continuance of a mental and soul activity.

**Q-3.** *For what purpose was this power given to her?*

**A-3.** That there might be given, as it were, the opportunity for the soul to use that it had builded within itself to make for a manifestation in a material world of those influences that are without and within. For, as has been given, the spirit maketh alive—and the kingdom of truth and light is within. With the abilities that are manifested through this soul entity, of subjugation of the influences from the material or carnal influences of experience, making then for self a channel through which there may come those forces or sources from the source of *all* supply. For, the Father giveth ever the increase, whether in material things, mental understanding or spiritual comprehension of that which is within thine own realm or ken.

When these then are used or abused, in such manners as to be used only for self-indulgences, self-aggrandizement, the fruits of these must be contention and strife, inharmony and the like.

As has ever been in all experiences, like begets like. For, the purposes, the desires, are both spiritual and carnal, and as to the soul development of same is as to what are the fruits of such activities. "By their fruits ye shall know them," whether they be of those that make for tares in the experiences of the souls of men, or whether they be of wheat or some other grain that maketh for an increase in the activities of such individuals in their associations with their fellow man. For, in the material world may there only be used in spirit that which creates for the spiritual life. And as ye do unto your fellow man, so may the activity of the individual be in that line, as to whether it fulfills those purposes for which it came into being, with those talents that have been developed through the experiences of the entity in its application of truth, life and understanding to material things.

**Q-4.** *How can Mrs. Garrett develop her ability to the highest degree?*

**A-4.** By keeping self in accord in the inner self with that which is the highest that may manifest itself through the abilities and faculties of the soul body. Thus may it give to the seeker, thus may it give to those that would knock; for, as He has promised ever, if ye seek in the light of thine understanding, trusting in Him for the increase, so may this attitude being kept ever within self make for self being that channel through which only the constructive influences may come into the experience of the seeker.

**Q-5.** *Do Mrs. Garrett's psychic powers depend on previous development? If so, describe the development which made this present manifested ability possible.*

**A-5.** As has been indicated, depends upon much that has been the soul development of the entity. And during those experiences when there were those in the lands now known as the Arabian and Persian, when there was the comprehension of the application of the truths in the spiritual relations of souls of men, with the constructive influences in the activities of individuals, during those days and periods when those activities known as the Zoroastrian were active in the peoples of the land. The entity then was not only an instructor, a teacher, one that gave much to aid peoples at that period when the fires of life had burned low, but the entity made for the awakening within the hearts and minds of many those relationships that should exist between the creative influences in the spiritual realms with the activities among men. Hence a guide, a teacher, that aided much in those experiences, aids in manifesting to those that seek to see materializations of those forces that would make for presenting of lessons, of tenets, of the various theses of understanding in the experiences of individuals.

**Q-6.** *Who are Mrs. Garrett's spiritual guides, and tell us something about them?*

**A-6.** Let them rather speak for themselves through that channel that is capable rather of presenting them in their light to that which has been the development of the soul itself in its experiences in the earth in the realms of their activity. For, their names are rather in *her* experience, in *her* seeking, than to find through other channels; even though they may be coming from the records that are made by each in their activity. Speak for thyself.

**Q-7.** *What counsel have you for Mrs. Garrett's spiritual development?*

**A-7.** Present self in thine own inner conscience in such a way and manner that answers for the conscience within self of its own soul development. And as the soul remains true to that which is its ideal from within, it may never give that other than constructive in its speech with those that seek to know the mysteries of soul and self-development; that has made for itself a channel through which men may approach those mysteries of life, and their activities in the minds, the hearts and the souls of men.

**Q-8.** *Is Mrs. Garrett contacting the highest possible sources for information in accordance with her development?*

**A-8.** As the soul seeks, higher and higher may be those influences of the activities in the experience for the *development* of others in *their* approach to such realms. When the soul seeks for self, for self's own protection and for self's own activities, it reaches the highest that is for that soul's development. When the self is open to those that would question or would counsel with, dependent upon the desire, the purposes, the aims, as to from what source or channel; as it does for *any* soul that has opened itself for the activities of those influences that are in and about a material world. Yet for the self, for the soul's protection, for the abilities, it seeks, it contacts that which is sufficient unto the needs of the soul in its development.

**Q-9.** *Is there any way in which Mrs. Garrett may be of special service to the work of Edgar Cayce?*

**A-9.** As their channels of activity cross or run one into another, in the various phases of experience, there may be those aids that will be for the common good of all. Rather than that it may aid any individual work as of Edgar Cayce or any other source. Rather those who give themselves (as both may be found to be doing) for the common good of mankind, as they merge in their efforts in these directions, may there be the aids rather one for the other. For, as has been given, in the union there is strength; whether this be applied in those things pertaining to the least in the earth or the greater in the realm of the spiritual activity. Hence, as each in clear purpose of desire to be of aid to their fellow man, not for self—but that the glory of God may be manifested in the hearts and souls of men, *thus* may each aid the other. For, as He has given, whether in body, in mind or spirit, ye come seeking to make known the love of the Father in the earth to the sons of men, ye may aid one another.

**Q-10.** *Would you explain why Edgar Cayce uses this method of hypnosis for going into trance?*

**A-10.** That as has oft been given, from the physical development or physical-mental development of the body, it has become necessary that there be the entire removal of the physical forces and physical attributes from the mental and spiritual and soul forces of the entity, to seek that through that built in the *soul*-body of the entity it may contact that which may be constructive in the experiences of those to whom such sources or such supplies of information may be brought.

**Q-11.** *How did it arise? Was it accident, or some entity or group suggest this plan?*

**A-11.** Soul development, rather. And the ability to, through those experiences in the earth in the varied activities, lay aside the consciousness that the soul and the spirit and the truth might find its way through to the seeker.

**Q-12.** *Do you suggest that trance is a useful method for help?*

**A-12.** Trance to the individual is as the necessary stimul(us) for each soul in its own development. There be those who may through their intuitive activity, that has subjugated the influences in the material, allow the mental soul to manifest. There be those who through looking into the past, or into the aura, or into all or any of those things that are as witnesses about every soul that walks through this vale. For, those that may lay aside the veil, in whatever form or manner, may make for the approach of aiding those in seeking to know that necessary in their development in the present experience.

**Q-13.** *If Edgar Cayce has ever had controls, does he know who they are?*

**A-13.** Anyone may speak who may seek, if the entity or the soul's activities will allow same; or if the desire of the individuals seeking so over commands as to make for a set channel.

**Q-14.** *Is Edgar Cayce clairvoyant in the hypnotic state?*

**A-14.** More so in the normal or physical state than in the hypnotic state; though *all* are one when in perfect accord with the universal forces from which the records of all activities may be taken.

**Q-15.** *If Edgar Cayce goes into trance without any control, could he not in a waking state get the inspiration direct?*

**A-15.** Not until there has been a more perfect cleansing of the carnal influences in the experiences of the soul, as has been indicated. With the regeneration that should come into the experience of the entity, this then may be the manner, the channel, the way through which much of constructive forces may be given.

**Q-16.** *What entity is giving this information now?*

**A-15.** Being directed, as has been indicated, from the records through Halaliel.

We are through.                                           507-1

# DEVELOPING PSYCHIC ABILITY

*by Henry Reed, Ph.D.*

There was once a monkey who discovered a jar of cherries. He stuck his hand in the jar and grabbed a handful of fruit. But when he went to withdraw his fistful of cherries, his engorged fist wouldn't fit through the opening of the jar. The monkey was stuck. The only way out of this trap was for him to release the cherries and then remove his opened hand—but he wanted the cherries and didn't want to let go.

What a paradoxical situation for the monkey! His wanting the cherries so much that he couldn't let go of them was the very thing that made it impossible for him to have them. How long will it take for the monkey to realize that by letting go of the cherries and removing his hand he will be able to pour *all* the cherries out of the jar?

This fable presents a predicament that often confronts us when we seek by force something that, in fact, will come to us only when we are willing to let go and receive it. The predicament arises from many different sources. Sometimes it is our need to be in control, to feel secure that by our own efforts we can guarantee certain results. Other times it comes about because our consciousness is caught in an ego trap, when we so desire something that we separate ourselves from that which we desire. It then *appears* to us that we must go after it, when all along it is already within us if we could only accept it.

What is the way out of the predicament of this ego trap? One useful principle—itself a paradox—is: "If you want something, then give it away—you can only really possess that which you can give away." Economic healing is an example of this principle, whereby persons realize material abundance by sharing what little they do have with others. Similarly, a paradoxical antidote to feeling lonely and unloved is to go outside ourselves to be friendly and loving to someone else. In its most fundamental version, this principle means, as expressed by Jesus, "For whosoever will save his life shall lose it: but whosoever will lose his life for my sake, the same shall save it." (Luke 9:24)

When it comes to developing psychic ability, the Edgar Cayce readings warn that a similar, ego-trap predicament awaits those who would "go for it" without the proper understanding of the necessity for "letting go of the goal." We may say to ourselves, "I want to learn how to read other people's minds, to learn how to see into the future. What techniques shall I employ to acquire these abilities?" On the surface, it seems like a straightforward proposition. A paradox exists, however, that will frustrate efforts or lead to unexpected or undesirable results. Sometimes the very nature of the way a person sets up a problem to be worked on makes the problem unsolvable. It is possible to conceive of psychic ability in such a manner that it becomes either impossible to develop or it develops in a regrettable manner.

Think for a minute what the psychic gift implies. Telepathy, clairvoyance, and precognition together imply a oneness, a unity among the various aspects of life. Time, space, and mind are not separating factors: Far away is here, tomorrow is now, you and I are one. Edgar Cayce, mystics, and philosophers have all been in agreement that there is an underlying unity to creation and that psychic events are an expression of this oneness.

Assume, then, that all information—including other people's thoughts, all past and future events—is a part of your being. You are totally psychic. How would you behave? By being concerned for others, by being of service and being concerned with the beautiful in life and what is uplifting to the spirit? In such a way you would naturally apply your psychic information to the betterment of all. But, giving no thought to yourself, you might never realize that you were psychic. Does that possibility disappoint you?

Suppose you wanted to know that *you* were psychic. Now you have a different motive. You would be looking for phenomena that would suggest that you were obtaining psychic information. However, that motivation would then deter you from a style of behavior that attunes you to the psychic, for you would no longer be attuned to the oneness of life but to your uniqueness. Or, if psychic phenomena continued to manifest through you, but you were now attributing to yourself qualities that really belong to the oneness of life, you would become "inflated."

Inflation is a term in psychology used to describe a prepsychotic state in which a person is haunted by delusions of truth, such as "I am the creator of my world." The truth is too much for such a person because he is confusing the personal "I" with the impersonal, universal "I AM." The person is full of spirit but is inflated by it because he is holding onto it as if it were his own possession, rather than letting it flow into the world at large, where it truly belongs. It sounds like a Catch-22 situation, similar to the one confronting the monkey with his hand in the cherry jar.

Edgar Cayce confronted this paradox. He manifested incredible psychic ability. Furthermore, from this psychic ability he discerned the fact that we are all psychic and are potentially capable of even greater feats than Cayce himself. How was he to explain this to us, knowing that if we were to "go for it"—attempting to put our hand in the jar of cherries—we might get stuck?

The main advantage Cayce had over us in developing his ability was that he didn't ask to be psychic. He didn't start out by sticking his hand in the cherry jar. His gifts began to manifest of themselves, perhaps as a result of his praying to be of help to sick children. The first sick child whom he was allowed to help was himself. As he became aware of this talent, he used it to help others. His psychic talent became a medium of expression for spiritual upliftment, taking its true role as a channel for the realization of oneness. In his personal life, he was a follower of the teachings of Jesus and spent his talents accordingly. His keen sense of humor kept him humble, as humor—not taking ourselves so seriously—is probably the most down-to-earth, human means of dealing with the paradoxical cherry jar of spiritual aspirations. So what did he do when he was confronted with the task of explaining the development of psychic ability?

June, 1932, was the occasion of the First Annual Congress

of the Association for Research and Enlightenment. For this first Congress, a featured event was Edgar Cayce giving a lecture. The title of his lecture was "How to Develop Your Psychic Powers." What was he to say? "Well, I slept on my spelling book—why don't you try it," or "Well, I lost my voice and no one could help me, so I went into trance, learned how to cure myself, and became psychic. The next time you get sick, try going into trance," or "I had a conversation with an angel and she told me what to do. Go talk to angels"? What was he to say?

What Cayce did was to give himself a reading. About three weeks before Congress, on two mornings, Cayce took time to have his psychic source respond to the task at hand. The lecture that resulted from this two-part reading (5752-1, -2) is well known and has appreared in many forms (one of which was in the July, 1982, issue of *The A.R.E. Journal* commemorating the 50th Anniversary Congress).

When in trance, Cayce was given this suggestion, "You will please outline fully the information which Edgar Cayce, present in this room, should give in lecture form on the subject 'How to Develop Your Psychic Powers,' to be given during the Congress . . ." (5752-1) What resulted was a very readable and clear message concerning the development of the psychic, a message that Cayce followed very closely in the resulting lecture.

In the first section of the reading, we learn certain basic assumptions concerning the development of psychic ability. We learn that we all have this ability latent within us, so that what is developed is the awakening of a "sleeping" rather than the development of a "new" talent. We also learn that in the unfoldment of *any* talent more is involved than simply the development of the talent itself: Development of the talent requires the growth of the person's *self*. Finally, we discover that most sensory talents, including the "sixth sense," involve aspects of the soul.

The reading begins by stating that the first order of business is to define the nature of the psychic and how it operates within a human being, so that we can see how it might be developed. To see what it is that is actually being developed, the definition is approached by looking at examples of other talents. Training requirements for a prizefighter, a musician, and an artist are used as examples to consider. Each of them must follow certain rules, and the development of their particular faculty will follow a certain course. But what is being trained? Something more than simply muscular strength, endurance, auditory and visual acuity, finger dexterity, and other peripheral skills is involved. The development of the self is required. It is as if we were to say that one cannot simply get newer and fancier tires for one's car and expect to experience the improved performance they will contribute to the car without also educating the driver and teaching modified driving techniques.

First of all, the reading would have us realize that we all have the psychic faculty and that it can be awakened in us.

**When one, then, is to develop a faculty, or a force, that is present—as any of these referred to, lying latent in one form or another in *every* individual; so, then, do the psychic forces, the psychic faculties, lie dormant or active in every individual, and await only that awakening or arousing, or the developing under those environs that make for the accentuation of same in the individual.**

Next, he would have us appreciate the nature of this psychic ability. It is a skill of perception, like the senses, and, like all the other senses, its functioning is interrelated to activities at the soul level of our being. How is this so? The reading explains, "As the psychic forces are manifesting, or do manifest through the senses, or those portions of the physical being that are trained for acuteness," these perceptions are obtained through activity at the soul level. The reading continues, "The psychic, then, is of the soul, and it operates through faculties of perception, whether hearing, seeing, feeling, or any portions of the sensory system . . . the brain . . . (the) glands . . ."

**In psychic forces we find the subconscious mental forces as a means, or manner of expression. Subconscious, we know, also partakes both of that which is a physical dormant consciousness and of the spiritual, or that upon which the body has fed through its activity in a material plane, and is a portion then of the soul of the entity.**

In his lecture, Cayce explained it thus: Perception operates through the senses, yet at the same time it requires an inner acuity, a faculty that is actually of the soul. ". . . in perception we develop the power or ability to discern with the faculty we possess." How do we hear music? Is it simply a matter of the physical transmission of sound waves? No, there is also something within us that reaches out and interprets the physical information, that makes "music" out of the physical event. Imagine listening to the beat of a clock. As it ticktocks monotonously along, we hear first one rhythm, then another. We can be amazed to discover the different rhythms we are able to hear. Yet we realize that we are not really "hearing" these different rhythms, for they are not really "out there" to be heard. Rather, we are "supplying" these rhythms to the physical event. Within us we have the faculty of "rhythm" and this faculty is of the soul—it is a timeless quality of our being. So, too, when we speak to others, how do they know what we mean by our words? Cayce asserts in his lecture that the meaning is partially conveyed psychically.

In the chapter, "The Sleeping Talent," it was explained how Cayce viewed the interaction of the psychic forces with the sensory processes in the body. Intuition or the "sixth sense" was seen as silently operating in all of our perceptions. Awakening this dormant talent is not so much a matter of increasing its activity as of increasing our *awareness* of our use of it.

This first reading ends with a warning. Having explained that the psychic forces are part of our being, both at the soul and at the physical level, the reading reminds us then that the psychic information we would channel will be affected by how we live our lives and by the type of thoughts we entertain about ourselves and the world. If we develop sensitivity but live negatively, that sensitivity could turn on us and bite us.

> **Much in the manner that a trained physical body may be raised to such power as to meet any antagonist, yet allowed to become unstable— through associations or derangements of the physical body, by the abusing of those laws that govern those portions of the system—is easily defeated, and loses that for which it has trained itself.**

The reading warns us, then, to create an ideal for ourselves as we begin to develop, or awaken, our psychic talent.

> **So, the warnings are that these forces, these activities, are to have their criterion from which a**

**premise may be made, and the judgment that is brought to a material condition may be seen as to how it may operate.**

In other words, we do not simply say to ourselves, "I'll take this psychic ability and make good use of it and do only good things." Instead, at a more basic level, he is telling us to take as part of our ideal the correct understanding of *how* the psychic operates. This is more like saying, "I allow my oneness with creation to express itself through psychic channels." With the first attitude, we "grab" on to psychic ability and "use" it; with the second, we "allow" the psychic forces to express their origin in oneness.

Cayce puts psychic ability in its place. It is no different from other aspects of the creative forces: creativity, love, sexual and procreative ability. It is all of these and they are of one source; developing one develops the others. This development occurs through the self's greater awareness that these aspects originate in the soul.

**In the warnings, there are seen many may be gotten from that which might be given in the development of *any* faculty or attribute of the physical or mental body; for the developments of the psychic forces are the development of the *spiritual* body, which manifests in and through the physical or mental body.** 5752-2

The second reading begins with a discussion of developing psychic ability in children. It seems to use this topic as a means of driving home the point about the importance of grounding psychic talent in ideals, and it poses the question as to whether psychic ability should be developed in children.

**Should one have children become acquainted with their Maker, or their selves? Would one have them be on speaking terms with the cosmic forces, with those influences that magnify the spiritual life?**

Thus it reminds us of how basic to our creation is the psychic. How can we say no?

**When would one begin, then, to teach or train children? Many months even before there is the conception, that the influence is *wholly* of the Giver of good and perfect gifts.**

The reading refers to the story of Hannah and her son Samuel. Hannah had been barren until she prayed to God and asked for a son whom she could dedicate to His service. The Cayce source would have us follow Hannah's example. Beyond the literal meaning here—praying for our children even before they are conceived—the reading is subtly reminding us that before we even begin to conceive of developing our psychic ability, we need to dedicate that talent to the Lord—that is, to the love of oneness.

How we think about the psychic faculty will influence whether and how it will operate in our lives. The reading now addresses the problem of the limitation of the rational mind and how it defeats the operation of this faculty.

> **What shall I read? Wherewithal shall I be clothed? Where shall I dwell? What shall I eat? and the like, become the questions of many. He that taketh thought of such has *already* limited the powers that influence through those forces in life.**

In his lecture, Cayce spends quite a bit of time explaining the signficance of that passage. He points out that, in contrast to the finite mind, the infinite mind cannot be known through reason: "We can comprehend the Infinite only by a faculty that is superior to reason. That faculty is the psychic force. One must enter a state in which the finite self no longer exists!" He goes on to lament the fact that we have lost, for the most part, the ability to drop our outer, finite selves. We have become so caught up in our concerns for our material well-being that we have "forgotten there is still an association of our soul with its Maker. That association is what we may choose to term *psychic forces* or psychic abilities."

What a different conception Cayce gave us of the psychic. It is the association of the soul with its Maker!

We need to remember that association, then, to start us on the right track as we develop *all* of those expressions of the creative, psychic forces. Having remembered that, what next? The reading indicates that one should be prepared not to grab the psychic force greedily, but rather to *express* it, to channel it toward a purpose.

> **How develop the psychic forces? So live in body, in mind, that self may be a channel through which the Creative Forces *may* run. How is the current of life or of modern science used in the commercial world? By preparing a channel through which same may run into, or through, that necessary for the use in the**

**material things. So with the body mentally, physically, spiritually, so make the body, the mind, the spiritual influences, a channel—and the *natural* consequence will be the manifestations.**

That is to say, rather than asking to become telepathic, ask instead to serve, to be useful—and if telepathy would help in that endeavor, so be it! This advice echoes our earlier thoughts on the predicament of the monkey whose hand was full of cherries but stuck in the jar. We have there the image of the hand inflated with its cherries, symbolic of a self-image inflated with notions of "its" abilities. We have also the image of the jar *pouring* out its cherries into an opened hand, and we are reminded of Cayce's phrases concerning the *current* of life, of our being a *channel* through which this current may flow.

This is similar to the adage, "Necessity is the mother of invention." That is to say, do not develop psychic ability for its own sake, but rather for the purpose of serving the spiritual. This advice has been well justified in parapsychology experiments conducted by A.R.E. It has been found that people evidence less telepathic ability when their ability is tested simply for its presence than when it is challenged to produce something needed to help another person. In the first instance, people are tested to determine if they can "read" another person's mind. If they can, they score a "hit." In this instance, the focus is on the subjects' abilities. In the second test, people are asked to determine what would be *helpful* for the target person, and their intuitive faculties are naturally brought to bear. The focus here is on being helpful and the psychic ability manifested is greater—and feels better!

Given, then, that we properly understand the nature of the psychic faculty and dedicate its development to the expression of our spiritual oneness, how might we best proceed to activate our psychic talent?

**Let that mind be in you as was in Him who thought it not robbery to make Himself equal with God, yet took on Himself the burden of all, that through His physical suffering, His privation in body, in mind, there might come the blessings to others. Not self, but others. He, or she, that may lose self, then, for others, may *develop* those faculties that will give the greater expression of psychic forces in their experience.**

In the words of his lecture, let's allow Cayce to explain that passage in the most human of terms:

"The adherence to and developing of the ability to see and appreciate the beautiful, the pure, and the lovely in everything and everybody we contact—everything within the scope of what affects our body, mind and heart—will develop in us the abilities to be in closer attunement with the Infinite. And this is developing our psychic abilities within."

# Reading Number 5752-1 ____

*This psychic reading given by Edgar Cayce at his home on Arctic Crescent, Virginia Beach, Va., the 8th day of June, 1932 . . .*

*Mrs. Cayce: You will please outline fully the information which Edgar Cayce, present in this room, should give in lecture form on the subject of "How to Develop Your Psychic Powers," to be given during the Congress of the Association for Research and Englightenment during the week of June 27th.*

Mr. Cayce: As in the approach to such a subject, well that we first define psychic phenomena and that through which same operates in the physical man, that we may know how or why such forces, or phenomena, might be developed in an individual.

When one develops muscle and brawn for the ring, or for any activity of such nature, there are certain rules of living that must be adhered to, or that have been found to be necessary for such an one to adhere to.

When a faculty of the body, as a pianist, or cornetist, or an artist, is to be developed, there are certain courses of development, certain training through which the body-physical, the body-mental, shall pass as *training* self for such an undertaking.

When one, then, is to develop a faculty, or a force, that is present—as any of these referred to, lying latent in one form or another in *every* individual; so, then, do the psychic forces, the psychic faculties, lie dormant or active in every individual, and await only that awakening or arousing, or the developing under those environs that make for the accentuation of same in the individual.

As the psychic forces are manifesting, or do manifest through the senses, or those portions of the physical being that are trained for acuteness, as is one that would be trained for art in the applying or the mixing rather of color, as one that gets the color, or the tone from the violin, or the like, these are percepts of faculties of the sensory organism, and are akin to the soul.

The psychic, then, is of the soul, and it operates through faculties of perception, whether hearing, seeing, feeling, or any portions of the sensory system; and those portions of the physical organism, as we know, that find their basis in the honored or dishonored portion of the physical organism—as those of the brain, those of the percepts that deal with glands that function with concept, conceptive thought, constructive thought—or destructive thought, dependent upon that it is fed upon. Much in the manner that a trained physical body may be raised to such power as to meet any antagonist, yet allowed to become unstable— through associations or derangements of the physical body, by the abusing of those laws that govern those portions of the system—is easily defeated, and loses that for which it has trained itself. This we see would follow throughout the whole length and breadth of a developing organism.

In psychic forces we find the subconscious mental forces as a means, or manner of expression. Subconscious, we know, also partakes both of that which is a physical dormant consciousness and of the spiritual, or that upon which the body has fed through its activity in a material plane, and is a portion then of the soul of the entity. Hence we find this development depends not only upon one of the experiences, though one experience may make for such an alteration that the activities of the soul, of the mental, of the physical, may be altered so as to be going in the opposite direction from that it has been going in the first premise.

So, the warnings are that these forces, these activities, are to have their criterion from which a premise may be made, and the judgment that is brought to a material condition may be seen as to *how* it may operate.

We are through for the present.                                        5752-1

# Reading Number 5752-2 _____

*This psychic reading given by Edgar Cayce at his home on Arctic Crescent, Virginia Beach, Va., the 9th day of June, 1932 . . .*

Mrs. Cayce: *You will please continue with the information which Edgar Cayce, present in this room, should give in lecture form on the subject "How to Develop Your Psychic Powers," to be given during the Congress of the Association for Research and Enlightenment during the week of June 27th.*

Mr. Cayce: In the warnings, there are seen many may be gotten from that which might be given in the development of *any* faculty or attribute of the physical or mental body; for the developments of the psychic forces are the development of the *spiritual* body, which manifests in and through the physical or mental body.

Then, as to the question of how to develop the psychic forces in an individual body:

How may one train children—*should* one train children—in such directions? *Should* one have children become acquainted with their Maker, or their selves? Would one have them be on speaking terms with the cosmic forces, with those influences that magnify the spiritual life? When one answers such, *some* would term this something of blasphemy, were this considered from much of the old or the period of orthodox thinking, as it has been termed. Rather may it be said that is the thinking of those that would have others think as they think, others feel as they feel. God speaks rather to *everyone!* Whosoever will may learn of Him.

As has been said, there should ever be the criterion, the measuring stick by which all such phenomena may be measured. Would many see the visions that were experienced by the man of old who walked close with God, they would be called extremists (as a mild term), devils, and those that walk with unseen forces; yet there should ever be held the will of the *Father* concerning the influences. Study as to how Hannah consecrated the life of her son to the service of Jehovah, how that he was under the influence of the law in every respect and tutored by one who was unable to (or did not, at least) tutor his own. What was the difference? The consecration of the body yet unborn! When would one begin, then, to teach or train children? Many months even before there is the conception, that the influence is *wholly* of the Giver of good and perfect gifts.

How develop the psychic forces? So live in body, in mind, that self may be a channel through which the Creative Forces *may* run. How is the current of life or of modern science used in the commercial world? By preparing a channel through whch same may run into, or through, that necessary for the use in the material things. So with the body mentally, physically, spiritually, so make the body, the mind, the spiritual influences, a channel—and the *natural* consequence will be the manifestations.

How best, then, to develop those latent forces in one *now*, those who have reached the years of maturity or responsibility in self? Let that mind be in you as was in Him, who thought it not robbery to make Himself equal with God, yet took on Himself the burden of all that through His physical suffering, His privation in body, in mind, there might come the blessings to others. Not self, but others. He, or she, that may lose self, then, for others, may *develop* those faculties that will give the greater expression of psychic forces in their experience.

What shall I read? Wherewithal shall I be clothed? Where shall I dwell? What shall I eat? and the like, become the questions of many. He that taketh thought of such has *already* limited the powers that influence through those forces in life. The *natural* things, as known and given, are the things that make for the better physical body in normal activity. *Normalcy,* not extreme in any manner! and there will be shown thee day by day that which will be the necessary for thine *own* development. To some certain amount of exercise, certain amounts of rest, certain amounts of various characters of breathing, of purification, of prayer, of reading—as is found necessary; but of *all* be true to that thou promiseth that source from which all health, all aid, must come! Don't fool yourself; for you *cannot* fool your Maker, and if there is fooling it is yourself— for your brother will soon find you out!

We are through for the present.                    5752-2

# A BLUEPRINT FOR THE NEW YEAR

*by Lynn Sparrow*

Any time in the year is a good time for new beginnings. No matter where we are on the calendar, we can always take an appraising look back over our shoulders and then peer optimistically forward to the 12 months stretching out ahead of us. For the A.R.E. member, new resolutions concerning meditation and other spiritual disciplines are likely to have their place right alongside the more "secular" resolutions to lose weight, quit smoking, or clean the attic. But do we realize just how deeply our individual ideals and purposes contribute to a group consciousness that in turn affects us?

## A.R.E. as a Model of Group Consciousness

It's no accident that A.R.E. was founded as an *association*. Consider the definition of the word: "an organization of persons having common interests, purposes, etc." (*Webster*) The readings of Edgar Cayce did not take this concept of common purposes lightly. As we can see in reading 254-95, given in June of 1937 for the Sixth Annual Congress of the Association for Research and Enlightenment, there is a great emphasis on the important part each one of us plays in creating the whole entity we call A.R.E. Like a mirror, that whole then reflects its influence back to us. Let's consider this reading—as well as the context in which it was given—in greater detail.

The annual membership Congress is an "A.R.E. New Year"

of sorts, for to this day it is a time when members and staff meet together to evaluate the progress of the past year and to brainstorm ideas for the work in the coming months. The Congress members of '37 asked the same question that we would probably ask today, if we had Edgar Cayce on hand to give us a reading. They asked him for "such counsel and guidance as may be helpful in understanding and carrying forward the work for the coming year." The response Edgar Cayce gave then reaches to each one of us today, as we consider our spiritual purposes and the impact they will have on our own lives and the lives of others over the coming year. In fact, we might consider the advice in this reading to be a blueprint for the ultimate New Year's resolution!

**We are in control.** Few concepts are more motivating than the idea that we *can* make a difference, that our ideas *do* count, and that we are ultimately the masters of our fate. Having a sense of control over our lives is as exhilarating as helplessness is debilitating. We can speculate that this is why Edgar Cayce's source began with the emphatic reminder that each individual plays a crucial role in *any* organization:

> **As has been intimated and given, in the combi- nations of efforts by individuals in a given direction, there is first the creation—in the universal forces—of the body-mind of such an organization . . .**

While we may be tempted to assume that such influence is true only for "spiritual" associations like A.R.E. or a church, the reading is quick to point out that this process takes place whenever people pursue a common purpose, be it material or spiritual. By way of illustration, the reading suggests that such phrases as "the spirit of America" (which many tend to understand in a figurative sense) refer to a force that is real in the "realms beyond matter." We are told that such forces have as much "body" or tangible form as the minds contributing to them build!

What does this mean to us as we go about our daily lives? It means that we are powerful beings, with the capacity to effect change—in ourselves, on the job, at home, in our social circles, in our national consciousness, and in the work of enlightenment, wherever and however it may be taking place.

---

**Our influence transcends material barriers.** This power of ours to influence the various groups to which we belong is a deceptive thing, for it apparently operates whether we recognize it or not. The group of Congress delegates gathered in Virginia Beach that June of 1937 was told in their reading not to be fooled, that even those not present bodily were having their influence on the Association. "For what is the builder? *Mind!"*

That phrase central to the philosophy of the Edgar Cayce readings rings out again, reminding us that we are dealing with a creative capacity that operates outside the confines of time and space. Do we feel "too far away" from A.R.E. headquarters? From the boardroom of the company for which we work? From our nation's capitol? When "mind is the builder," there is no such thing as distance. The "body-mind" of any group purpose is as near as our own consciousness.

**We begin to participate as soon as we join with others.** Still there may be a tendency to feel that we must be well established in a group or organization before we can have an effect. Most of us at one time or another have known the peculiar sense of alienation that comes with being a new member of a group that already has a momentum of its own. This experience can come in many forms: Perhaps you've recently married into a family; taken a new job; joined a new church; moved into a new neighborhood; joined a new club or civic group; enrolled in a new school. As much as you may believe that mind is the builder, somehow it seems that your ability to really *contribute* to this group consciousness will be activated only after you're no longer an "outsider."

Yet, if we can draw a parallel from that 1937 Congress reading, our influence is felt from the moment we join any given group. The reading states that with the incoming of new members, new directions for the organization were being formed. The formative effect of these new members would first be felt in the "soul" of the organization, the reading says, and then later some of those new members would go on to direct the organization through leadership roles.

The message here is clear: Once we become part of *any* group consciousness, our influence is being added to the whole. There is never a time when any individual is an "unimportant" part of A.R.E. or of any other group effort.

**Creative power brings responsibility.** It can be a heady experience to realize—to really *know* deep within—that we are active, creative participants in the world around us, transcending material boundaries and hierarchies to have our influence. It can also be a sobering stare into the face of responsibility, for our potential to be a non-constructive influence goes hand in hand with our power to create realities in the "body-mind" of the groups to which we belong.

When Cayce's Congress reading emphasizes the formative influence each member has, a warning is given in the same breath: "*Do not* deviate from your ideal!" As we consider the year ahead, we need to recognize the tremendous creative power that operates within us—with or without our conscious direction, with or without the guiding force of an ideal. It has been suggested that there are no "idle" thoughts, that we are building our future—individually and collectively—with the thoughts that we hold. If we wish to participate constructively in our world over the coming year, it will be important to commit (or recommit) ourselves to an ideal.

# Re-examining Our Ideals

What should we, as spiritual seekers and members of an association seeking to bring light into the world, hold as our ideal? What concept or principle should we use to direct our contributions to the "body-mind" of our families, neighborhoods, churches, workplaces? How simple it would be if we could turn to a page in the Cayce readings and see the "ideal" ideal articulated in black and white! Yet one of the great strengths of this material is its tolerance and even celebration of diversity, its insistence that all individuals must set their own ideals according to their own best understanding of what is good.

**Looking for the good.** We may infer from the reading under consideration that the ideals we hold for our family life, our community activities, our jobs, our involvement in A.R.E. over the coming year should be rooted in our personal understanding of the good within these structures.

In one form or another, these ideals will reflect our commitment to bringing this good into greater manifestation. They will be our way of saying, "I choose to be an agent of growth within this group consciousness, to do my part to enlarge the good that I see within this association of people." Consider the following advice, for example:

**Hold fast to that which you experience in your own relationships with your body, your mind, your fellow man; and present to others that (which) *you* have found to be good.**

Given this reading's earlier reference to the group's mental creation of a "soul," even in material organizations, we might speculate that it would always be important to hold fast to the good that we find in any endeavor.

This is not to say that we should withhold our support from any group effort unless we can see *only* good being accomplished. How many of our social, organizational, and economic structures would measure up to so rigid a criterion? The spirit of this reading seems to suggest, rather, that we look for those aspects of an organization which we have found to be good in our own experience. If such an organization or group also has weaknesses, we should not be blind to them; but neither should we let a recognition of the weaknesses dim our view of the good aspects.

**The good is found in the mundane.** For those who gathered to hear that 1937 Congress reading, the sleeping Cayce provided some guidelines for evaluating the helpfulness or the value of his psychic work in their own lives: Don't look for the unusual or the "shocking," he told them. We can well imagine how, in the face of the marvelous psychic feats Cayce was able to perform, those early enthusiasts must have been tempted to try to "shock" people into acceptance of the work. Edgar Cayce was demonstrating on a daily basis a power that to some would be nothing short of miraculous. It was only natural that his friends and supporters would want to spotlight the sheer miraculousness of his gift in order to convince more people of its value.

Yet he told them to focus instead on more mundane considerations. What changes had the information in the readings brought in the daily lives of individuals? How had they, personally, been affected? In what ways had these effects been passed along to their neighbors, to everyone else they contacted day by day? The real value of the Cayce readings was (and continues to be) in the constructive influence they might have on people—physically, mentally, and spiritually.

Before we rush past this concept as one we've heard many times before in the Cayce readings, let's consider its implications. How many times do we fail to see the value in an organization or group because we are looking for good in the extraordinary rather than in the ordinary process of daily living? It is easy to feel spiritually thwarted in a job that involves filing invoices or selling clothing or managing an industrial plant. It is easy to overlook the growth going on in a family structure when its members do not all consciously hold to a spiritual ideal. It is easy to assume that a Saturday night social gathering has less real value than a prayer meeting. In short, it is easy to compartmentalize our lives into "secular" and "spiritual" categories, overlooking the divine expression in the everyday fabric of life. Yet it is in the day-by-day experiences that we *live* life, and nowhere is it more important than when we exercise our capacity for constructive influence.

To summarize thus far, then: We are powerful beings who, together with others in *all* of our social structures, shape the world around us. Our influence operates outside of physical barriers and regardless of whether we make that influence constructive or destructive. Our influence will be constructive so long as it is rooted in an ideal or our best understanding of the good within these structures. We need to recognize and express that good in the ordinary experiences of daily living.

The next segment of reading 254-95 explores a world view that will allow us to recognize and express this good.

## An Orientation for Constructive Living

Our ability to recognize and augment the good in the world around us depends to some degree upon our concept of ultimate good. Once we perceive a universe that is good, orderly, and purposeful, we can begin to see those qualities reflected in the people around us and in the structures they create in order to work toward common purposes. Whether those purposes are focused on material sustenance, recreation, fulfillment of emotional needs, mental development, or spiritual growth, we can recognize the reflections of an ultimate benevolence in the universe. Nowhere in the Cayce readings do we find this concept more beautifully expressed than in the reading at hand:

> **The startling thing to every soul is to awaken to the realization that it is indeed a child of God! That is startling enough for any man, any woman, any being, in this sin-sick world!**

At first this reference to a "sin-sick world" may seem to be at loggerheads with the idea of holding fast to the good. But on closer examination, it is consistent with the readings' overall philosophy. Take, for example, their approach to physical health. The readings assert that balance and wellness are our natural state. Yet they don't suggest that we deny the reality of illness. Instead, they provide very practical suggestions for re-establishing wellness, beginning with attitudinal orientation and leading right on through physical health care measures.

Just so, the readings describe a natural state of wellness and balance on the spiritual level, while at the same time recognizing the existence of spiritual sickness. The very use of the phrase, "sin-sick," suggests that this is an unnatural state of affairs, one from which we desire release. The prescribed antidote begins with an attitudinal reorientation—to awaken to the realization that we are children of God. This is an orientation that we can carry into the New Year. It is an attitude we can employ in order to amplify the divine expression in our human social structures.

**God is personal and universal.** The readings frequently use terms like "Creative Forces" to describe God. This has led some to assume that Edgar Cayce's source was suggesting the existence of an impersonal God, a kind of universal energy devoid of personal qualities. But for every reading that calls God "Creative Forces," there is another that presents a deity with all the personal attributes of a loving parent. The reading we have been following is one such case.

In it we are told that God is "mindful" of us, that He continuously calls us to be His children, and that He is a loving Father who cares. So personal is each individual's relationship with his or her God that the reading likens it to the monogamy of a marriage. A unique, one-on-one relationship with the God of the universe is the heritage of *every* soul—some have already experienced it, while others still have the realization ahead of them. "That is thy message!" we are reminded.

What is our "message" if not the orientation that we carry with us into all of our activities and contacts with other people? While it may not always be appropriate to express our "message" in words, it is an orientation that will shape the "body-mind" of each group to which we belong. For if we truly believe that our co-workers, friends, and family members are, like us, children of a loving God, that belief will allow us to see and emphasize the God-like qualities in all of our endeavors together. From the perspective of the reading under study, this orientation is a cornerstone of constructive living.

**Can anything, any experience, any condition be more worthwhile? That, though there are those things that make men afraid, there are turmoils in this or that direction in the relationships of human experience that may terrify thee for the moment, there is *HE* who cares! And He may walk and talk with *THEE!***

When we are inclined to feel that the turmoil and uncertainties of our time make it difficult to hold to the good, we need to remember that the words above were spoken to a world in the throes of the Great Depression and as the momentum of World War II was steadily building. Part of our "message," then, should be that the promise is good through all time, under all circumstances.

**Evaluating life's messages.** It is not enough, though, for us to know what *our* message is. We encounter many messages every day—on our televisions, in the conversations of our friends and associates, through the various philosophical and religious teachings we may hear. If we absorb these messages without discrimination, they subtly become a part of our outlook; and soon we are helping to build those orientations into all of the "body-minds" in which we participate. It is important, then, to evaluate the messages we encounter—in order to consciously choose the mental orientation we build.

The reading suggests a criterion for our evaluation: "They that deny that He hath come in the flesh are not worthy of acceptation." Is Edgar Cayce's source making a doctrinal statement here? Is it suggesting that we should accept or reject a message on the basis of dogma? If so, this statement is jarringly inconsistent with the rest of the philosophy in the readings, which declines to make cut-and-dried, doctrinal judgments. But if this is instead a reference to Jesus' ultimate example of divine expression in the material world, then we are dealing with a principle quite consistent with what has gone before. Those who deny His coming in the flesh are not so much rejecting a doctrine as they are failing to see God expressing Himself in human form.

**Partnership with Jesus.** Whenever we deny His coming in the flesh by failing to see the opportunity for expressing the Divine, we are also missing out on a special partnership. For this reading goes on to suggest that in Jesus' overcoming the world, He is in a position to offer us a share in His victory. We are invited to "Drink from that fountain that He builds in the minds, the hearts, the souls of those that seek to know Him . . ." We can understand this invitation in terms of the "body-mind" concept discussed earlier. Jesus' overcoming made such a change in the overall "body-mind" of mankind that each one of us can share in the frame of mind that Jesus held when He manifested the Divine in a material world.

Just as we have our influence on every group consciousness that will in turn reflect its influence back to us, our partnership with Jesus is a two-way relationship. We are told in this reading that He has entrusted the world into our care. We are challenged to make a decision: "What will you do about Jesus and His trust *in you*?" How often do we think about His trusting *us*? Yet once again, our inescapable responsibility stares us in the face. A trust has been placed in each one of us to be His partners in bringing divine expression into the flesh and the structures of the world. How do we do this? "Be gentle, be kind, be patient . . . claim Him as thy brother . . ."

**Take part in the leavening process.** We need to begin to do our part now, rather than waiting for some great mission to unfold for our lives. For, "you are only fooling

yourselves if you are not giving, doing, being, even thy little!"
Our "little" contribution to the "body-minds" of the groups
of society to which we belong may seem meager to us. But
recent research bears witness to the awesome power of a
few committed individuals: When a group of meditators
gathered daily for a brief period of attunement in a high-
crime area of a major American city, the neighborhood's
"body-mind" responded and crime decreased dramatically.

By joining with a few others who are willing to do their
"little" parts, we too can discover that "it is not numbers that
count, for it is the leaven that leaveneth the lump!" Each one
of us, doing our little in the coming year, has the capacity to
transform the circles we move in, the world we live in.

# Reading Number 254-95 ___

*This psychic reading given by Edgar Cayce at his home
on Arctic Crescent, Virginia Beach, Va., the 30th day of
June, 1937, in accordance with those present at the Sixth
Annual Congress of the Association for Research and
Enlightenment, Inc. . . .*

*Mrs. Cayce: You will have before you the Association for
Research and Enlightenment, Inc., as it studies and
presents the psychic work of Edgar Cayce. You will give for
those assembled here for the Sixth Annual Congress such
counsel and guidance as may be helpful in understanding
and carrying forward the work for the coming year.*

Mr. Cayce: Yes, we have the ideals, the purposes of the
Association for Research and Enlightenment, Inc., together
with the desires, the motives, the purposes of those
gathered here in reference to same.

First, we would give a message to those of the Directorate
of the Association at this time:

As has been intimated and given, in the combinations of
efforts by individuals in a given direction, there is first the
creation—in the universal forces—of the body-mind of such
an organization; no matter of what nature, be it physical,

material, or for spiritual purposes. It grows to be—with the activities of such a group, association, combination, body-mind; and the purposes that you term soul—which is in the stellar forces rather its association of combination with such.

Hence you speak of the spirit of America, of Germany, of the Nordic people, of the Mayan, of the Celtic, or whatnot. These are influences that have taken shape in the realms beyond matter, yet influence same, with as much of a body as the mind (the builder) has builded.

So with your Association, you are taking body, soul. With the incoming of the present members you are forming policies, you are forming purposes. *Do not* deviate from your ideal!

In the formation of same there are others that need to be and will become members of the directing group, or your Trustees—that form policies.

Many of you as individuals oft feel that those who have presented themselves bodily are not really interested or have not contributed to the welfare, the building up. This is not always true. For what is the builder? *Mind!*

In that giving in of self to same, then, you have gathered nearer to the correct group than heretofore.

Then, as the directing force, ask the more oft of all their intents, their prayers, their thoughts, as to the ways, the manners of presenting that which may be of a helpful, hopeful nature through the information that may be presented through your channel Edgar Cayce; and you will find that the Work, the Association, will take on new life.

These as we find are worthy of consideration by all who would direct, who would counsel, who would form policies, who would make for ideas and the adherence to the ideals—and the *courage* then to carry on.

As for those present in their seeking: First, as has so oft been given, determine within your own mind as to the reliability of the sources of information and of the information itself.

Hold fast to that which you experience in your own relationships with your body, your mind, your fellow man; and present to others that (which) *you* have found to be good. Not as one attempting to sway by proof, by verification, those that seek only for the gratifying of such. But if that being presented has a mind, has a soul, it is then indeed of divine origin.

These are determined by what you have seen the information from such a source produce in the life of individuals, in your own self, in your neighbor, in those with whom you have come in contact in one manner or another; and not through that of any nature that is to startle any group. The startling thing to every soul is to awaken to the realization that it is indeed a child of God! That is startling enough for any man, any woman, any being, in this sin-sick world!

And yet it is the heritage of every soul to awake to that consciousness that God indeed is mindful of the children of men, and calls ever. "If ye will be my children, I will be thy God."

This is the message, then, that you shall carry; for there is a loving Father that cares. That is thy message!

There *is;* for you have experienced it, you can and you may experience it in your own life!

Can anything, any experience, any condition be more worthwhile? That, though there are those things that make men afraid, there are turmoils in this or that direction in the relationships of human experience that may terrify thee for the moment, there is *HE* who cares! And He may walk and talk with *THEE!*

*That* ye may experience in thine *own* life!

*Do* that.

Then you know, then you find as to whether the messages that may be presented through such a channel as this are worthy of consideration—and by that standard ye shall judge.

For what was the judgment, what *is* judgment, what will ever be the judgment? They that deny that He hath come in the flesh are not worthy of acceptation. They that give thee that which is not helpful, hopeful, and patient and humble, and not condemning any, are not worthy!

This is thy judgment.

What, then, will you do with Jesus?

For He is the Way, He is the Light, He is the Hope, He *is* ready. Will you let Him into thy heart? or will you keep Him afar or apart? Will ye not eat of His body, of the bread of life? Drink from that fountain that He builds in the minds, the hearts, the souls of those that seek to know Him and His purposes with men, with the world!

For having overcome the world, He *indeed* has it—as it were—in the palm of His hand; and has entrusted to you this world, because of His faith, His love for you.

What will you do about Jesus and His trust *in you?*

As these, then, are the things that you have oft heard in one manner or another, they have become to some passé; they have become to others as "How can it be?"; they are to others still just a question. But "Try ye the spirits." Know those that know Him are in accord with that which is His purpose, His desire, with men.

Then, how may you as individuals in your various spheres of activity, in your walks of life among men that think not of Him, carry on? By just showing forth that He hath given. Though others may be unjust, rail not; for it indeed must be that these things come, but woe to them by whom they come!

Rather know that the meek, the patient, those that are of one mind in Him *shall—SHALL*—inherit the earth, the possessions thereof.

Learn ye what to do with them. For if you say, "Had I much, I would give to the poor; had I plenty I would be kind to the unfortunate," and you do not do the same with your mite you would not do it if you had much! What said He? "She that cast in the penny gave more than them all." So you are only fooling yourselves if you are not giving, doing, being, even thy little!

For as He has given, it is the leaven that leaveneth the whole lump.

Be gentle, be kind, be patient; for the earth is thy Lord's.

Do ye claim Him as thy brother, as thy friend, as thy neighbor?

Do that—for thy own sake, for His sake! So much He has given! What hast thou done?

For as ye do it unto the least of thy brethren, ye do it unto Him.

That is the law!

Ready for questions.

**Q-1.** *First, the general questions—[1210]. Is the source of this information a group source, an individual source, or a recorded source?*

**A-1.** As has so oft been given, this is rather of the universal. That which is recorded may be read. That which is written may be interpreted. That which is individual may be had. But it is also a constructive source, so only gives that which is helpful if it will be applied.

When an individual seeks for personal or bodily aid, it is part and parcel of that individual and is read by and through the real desire of the seeker.

When it is the Life source, it is recorded upon space and time—and is that which is to be kept against that day; for time and space are as the evolution upon which the forces of the Divine make for that change that brings same into the experience of those souls who seek to become one with the Creative Energies.

Hence *all* may be touched, *all* may be drawn upon. And, as has been given, if it were individualized by a guide, it would become limited; while if universal it is in the hands of Him that is the Maker, the Giver, the Creator. For, hath He not given, "Abide in me, as I in the Father, that I in the Father may be glorified in thee!" Ye that seek self-glory know its hardships. Ye that seek the glory of the Father know its beauties.

**Q-2.** *[1196]. Please give me practical suggestions for taking part in group work of the Ass'n in Montgomery, Ala., provided these sources feel I can be successful in such work.*

**A-2.** Take the Study Group Manual [262-100 Supplement], study same. Gather those one by one that are known as thee to be interested in knowing more of thy relationship to thy Maker, to thy brother; and here ye have thy group! Though it may be one, though it may be two—for years; it is not numbers that count, for it is the leaven that leaveneth the lump!

**Q-3.** *How can skepticism be met in relation to the work?*

**A-3.** Rather forget it! Live what ye know! Be ye *living* examples, known of men! For did not they in high places deny Him? These are living experiences, and are to be met with the smile and with the love as ye would have thy God show thee. Honest skepticism is a seeker. That which is self-knowledge and its own glory, forget.

**Q-4.** *[1100]. What is the best approach to strangers in relation to the work?*

**A-4.** Merely give "This I know by experience. You may have same if you seek. No one may attain same for you." For thy relationships to thy Creator are personal, not group, not relations. No wife would like for the husband to love many women. No man desires that many men love the wife, in the close relationships; but all as to God. That! "If you seek you may know. For it is a personal experience." And, as has been given, if it does not answer to that Divine within, it is not yet time. For how gave He when there was the call for a separation? The day is not yet fulfilled for the Hivites nor the Hittites, but their end is in sight. So as you approach those that know not, give only your personal experience, and "Take it or leave it, as it is."

But join you to the group that would direct the Association!

**Q-5.** *(689). How is the best way to cooperate with other organizations who are in sympathy with or who have an understanding of this work?*

**A-5.** As has so oft been given. Let those that are sincere, that are honest with themselves, seek not the differences in the organizations but where they may cooperate. And as they do, you will find—as with these that are gathered here, they are of many faiths, many creeds, yet they find one common purpose—*good* to thy fellow man! So, as those that have found in this vision, in this interpretation, or in that promotion or in that experience of this or that nature, seek rather the common interest where there *is* cooperation, rather than the differences. And then if any group, if any organization, if any association has not this, it has not the full soul . . .

254-95

# THE WORK OF EDGAR CAYCE TODAY

The Association for Research and Enlightenment, Inc. (A.R.E.®), is a membership organization founded by Edgar Cayce in 1931.

- 14,256 Cayce readings, the largest body of documented psychic information anywhere in the world, are housed in the A.R.E. Library/Conference Center in Virginia Beach, Virginia. These readings have been indexed under 10,000 different topics and are open to the public.

- An attractive package of membership benefits is available for modest yearly dues. Benefits include: a bi-monthly magazine; lessons for home study; a lending library through the mail, which offers collections of the actual readings as well as one of the world's best parapsychological book collections, names of doctors or health care professionals in your area.

- As an organization on the leading edge in exciting new fields, A.R.E. presents a selection of publications and seminars by prominent authorities in the fields covered, exploring such areas as parapsychology, dreams, meditation, world religions, holistic health, reincarnation and life after death, and personal growth.

- The unique path to personal growth outlined in the Cayce readings is developed through a worldwide program of study groups. These informal groups meet weekly in private homes.

- A.R.E. maintains a visitors' center where a bookstore, exhibits, classes, a movie, and audiovisual presentations introduce inquirers to concepts from the Cayce readings.

- A.R.E. conducts research into the helpfulness of both the medical and nonmedical readings, often giving members the opportunity to participate in the studies.

For more information and a color brochure, write or phone:

**A.R.E., P.O. Box 595**
**Virginia Beach, VA 23451, (804) 428-3588**